Tiny perfect
collection

Sarah Lugg's

THE HANDCRAFTED WEDDING

Special touches for the perfect day

Sterling Publishing Co., Inc. New York
A Sterling / Chapelle Book

Gros-Grain Français
Pattern BEAUVAIS
10 Yards
Col.
Made in France

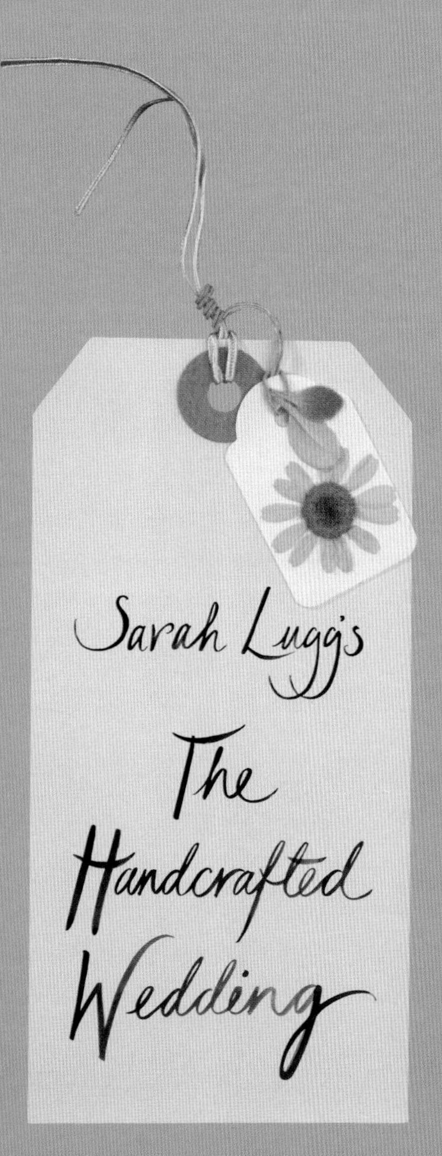
Sarah Lugg's
The Handcrafted Wedding

Chapelle, Ltd.: Jo Packham, Sara Toliver, Cindy Stoeckl

Art Director: Bo Hotston
Assistant Art Director: Karla Haberstich
Editoral Director: Patrick Regan
Graphic Illustrator: Kim Taylor
Copy Editors: Caroll Shreeve, Marilyn Goff
Photographers: Caroline Arber and Mo, Jim Pascoe

A source and supply list for the projects in this book can be found on Chapelle's web site. If you have any other questions or comments, please contact:
Chapelle, Ltd., Inc., P.O. Box 9252, Ogden, UT 84409
(801) 621-2777 • (801) 621-2788 Fax
e-mail: chapelle@chapelleltd.com
web site: www.chapelleltd.com

Library of Congress Cataloging-in-Publication Data available

10 9 8 7 6 5 4 3 2 1
Published by Sterling Publishing Co., Inc.
387 Park Avenue South, New York, NY 10016

Distributed in Canada by Sterling Publishing
c/o Canadian Manda Group, One Atlantic Avenue, Suite 105
Toronto, Ontario, Canada M6K 3E7
Distributed in Great Britain by Chrysalis Books
64 Brewery Road, London N7 9NT, England
Distributed in Australia by Capricorn Link (Australia) Pty. Ltd.
P.O. Box 704, Windsor, NSW 2756, Australia
Printed in China

Sterling ISBN 1-4027-0258-2

CONTENTS

In the studio, Spring 2002

INTRODUCTION

Congratulations! The fact that you're reading this book likely means that you are in the process of planning your wedding. I know from experience that this is an exciting, exhilarating, and sometimes daunting task.

As any bride-to-be knows, the local bookstore holds no shortage of voluminous wedding guides. What makes this one different, I think, is that it was created from the point of view of a visual artist—an artist whose own wedding is still fresh in memory. This book isn't intended to be an all-encompassing wedding encyclopedia filled with checklists, recipes, and tips on wedding etiquette. Rather, it is meant to be a creative wellspring and idea generator. Its dual purpose is to inspire—with gorgeous photos and creative ideas, and to instruct—with detailed points on how you can create custom touches for your own wedding.

The creative genesis for this book was my own wedding, and a good many of the projects that the book illustrates made their debut on that glorious day. In preparing for my wedding, I spent considerable time thinking about—and visualizing—the overall look or impression that I wanted to create on that day. I've come to think of this overall impression as a kind of "story." With tremendous help from many talented friends and family members, I was able to tell the story that I had visualized so clearly. The goal of this book is to help you put forth your own personal story on your wedding day.

I believe that, above all, your wedding should be yours. It should be an expression—and a celebration—of your own personal vision. So, while this book does offer specific instruction on more than 50 wedding projects, there is always room for customization within each project. Substitution, personalization, and straying from the mainstream are all strongly encouraged! My greatest hope is that this glimpse into my world will encourage and inspire you to create the wedding of your dreams—a wedding that is the perfect reflection of your own world.

OUR WEDDING

In 1999, while I was enjoying a year as Victoria magazine's artist-in-residence, I was caught up in another, even greater whirlwind of activity. I was planning my wedding. To my surprise and delight, Victoria ended up doing a feature story on the wedding. It came off beautifully—both the wedding and the story. The personal touches that I created for my own wedding seemed to strike a chord with many people. When one of those people (who happened to be in the book-publishing business) suggested to me that I might consider putting together a book of ideas on how to throw a uniquely beautiful wedding full of personal touches, I leapt at the chance.

The opportunity to do this book incorporates two of my favorite things. First, I adored every second of my own wedding including the planning and the preparation, and was tickled at the prospect of reliving the fun. And, second, I truly love all the delicate detail work inherent in creating these handmade wedding touches (that is, the invitations, flowers, favors, gifts, table décor, and such). It was for good reason, after all, that *The Times* (of England) once dubbed me "the goddess of small things."

The main reason that I had such fun preparing for my own wedding was the company I had in doing it. It enabled me to spend countless hours working on projects with my mother and three of my closest girlfriends—who very conveniently happened to be three of my most creative friends. This creative team completely indulged me. When the invitations I had envisioned included tiny, individually—stitched silk hearts on tags—all 52 of them—these amazing women stood undaunted with needles ready.

I do believe, upon reflection, that there were some things to which my mother and friends said no—otherwise we'd likely still be preparing for the wedding to this day. But, whatever it was that they talked me out of, I can't remember now, and there certainly wasn't anything lacking on the day. So, brides, take caution—you will tend to loosen the plot a bit in

your effort to make this day all you have dreamed. In all the rush of planning and activity, don't neglect to enjoy this time. It will go so quickly, both the lead up to your wedding and the day itself. The preparation can be very enjoyable, and a great bonding time between mother and daughter— and, of course, between the bride and her girlfriends.

I went back to the village where I grew up to get married. This was rather nice as the excitement from our family home flowed into village life. I was so lucky that my parents were very supportive but never controlling during the lead up to our wedding. They and their friends were wonderful, whether it was stripping their gardens for the perfect blooms or tracking down just the right silk for my wedding dress.

Many friends confided in us that the only regret they had about their wedding day was that it had passed so quickly, so we decided to extend the nuptial celebrations to a second day by having a cricket match. This not only enabled us to spend more time with our guests, but also to invite many friends and acquaintances whom we were unable to include in the previous day's celebration. We invited my new husband Robert's cricket team to play the "Sarah Lugg Eleven," a team made up of players from the wedding party. This was another wonderful day, less formal, and we were both more relaxed and able to enjoy a bit of casual time with our guests. Another nice thing about extending the celebration was that it enabled us to use the flowers that everyone had so exquisitely arranged for the previous day. We decorated the cricket pavilion and my parents' home, as everyone was invited back to the house for a barbecue after the cricket had finished.

The end of the two-day celebration found us all happily exhausted. In truth, after so many months of anticipation and preparation—especially the last few feverish days—the wedding day itself seemed leisurely by comparison. With the help and inspiration of so many treasured friends, our wedding was more than a girl could hope for—and everything I'd always dreamed.

HOW THIS BOOK IS ARRANGED

To best cover the range of projects in this book—and to fully illustrate the infinite variety of wedding touches you can create—I've settled on three distinct visual themes, or "stories," around which to build the projects.

These visual themes are Country Lanes, Color Brights, and Antique Whites. Within each of these stories, we'll show the entire range of wedding creations, including invitations, gifts and favors, decorative lights, floral arrangements, and other little surprises along the way.

The introduction to each of the three sections begins with a double-page "mood board." I created these mood boards to give a visual representation to the overall essence, or feeling, of each story. The boards are intended to inspire you to think visually, be creative, and be open-minded about your sources of inspiration.

I strongly encourage you to create a personal mood board when you begin planning your own wedding. Collect images from magazines and books and even add three-dimensional objects that appeal to you. Arrange these elements to your liking and affix them to a large sheet of cardboard or lay them out on a table. You'll find that it will help you forge a visual identity to your wedding and will help immensely when it comes to communicating your vision to florists, dress designers, caterers, photographers, or—if you are really lucky—the wedding planner.

Readers will find photographs of the completed projects in the front of the book and specific project "makes" with directions for preparation and presentation in the back.

Country Lanes
Memory Lanes
Tread with
care

Country Lanes

Dappled sunlit tables with lawn daisies as table numbers. Napkin rings and simple guest gifts and favors.

OVE AND CHERISH

COUNTRY LANES INSPIRATION

This story takes its inspiration from English Country Lanes with elements from the cottage garden. The flowers were natural choices, inspired by the hedgerow. I love the idea of using one flower; but playing around with the scale, and the daisy—with its myriad species—makes a perfect specimen for this kind of experimentation. Pictured here, tiny lawn daisies share the spotlight with huge oxeye daisies. The printed material in this mood board consists of old botanical prints of ferns and grasses, antique maps of the countryside, and old seed packets. Collected from the potting shed are antique plant tags, old terra-cotta pots and seed trays.

The location for your wedding and reception will have quite an impact on the overall tone of your day, and it is worth giving considerable thought. For this casual country wedding, the tables were set outside amongst the apple trees in a small orchard. The scale of the orchard was just right. Even though it was an open space, the leaves and branches of the trees offered some intimacy and a natural canopy. The natural ceiling was a perfect frame from which to hang the homemade tea-light lanterns, which were lit as the sun began to set.

Inspired by the many daisies in my lawn! Use actual turf or wheat grass from your flower market or health food store. Cut to size and nestle daisies in amongst the grass. You might also create the table number from shells or pebbles laid out on a bed of sand, make the numbers from small leaves and twigs arranged on a patch of moss, or outline the numbers in colorful flower petals set on a white china platter.

CARD RING: (upper left) This simple paper napkin ring was created by color-copying original artwork onto a cloth-textured heavy-weight paper.
RIBBON KNOT: (upper right) The ribbon was inspired by the stem of the daisy. For a more organic look, consider using a natural tie such as a palm frond.
BUTTON DAISY: (lower right) The contrast of the button's pale yellow luster against the crisp, white tissue-paper petals adds interest to this simple yet lovely ring.
METAL RING: (lower left) A small sprig of fresh herbs is neatly tucked into each napkin. Choose an herb that won't wilt quickly—good choices are rosemary (pictured), thyme, and bay.

Inspired by my collage, 'Gardener's Lore', holly, yew, and hornbeam saplings are wrapped in brown glassine and old ordnance survey maps. A nice idea is to use old maps of the area where you are getting married or of the areas where you and your partner were raised. The packages are adorned with tags made from antique postcards and maps, which in turn are decorated with pressed ferns and daisies, paper butterflies, and hand-stitched leaves. To save time, you might consider making a set of three or four images, then color-copying them.

As favors for the ladies or as place name cards, these seed packets are a perfect companion to the saplings. The seeds have been replaced with lime green dragées, but you might alternatively use chocolate-coated coffee beans or candied fruits. To get away from the food theme altogether, you might try tiny leaf- or flower-shaped soaps.

A N E M O N E

Color Brights

Clashing colors on and above the
table, with ribbons at the window.
Window dressing, table numbers
and favors, place names and
napkin rings.

COLOR BRIGHTS INSPIRATION

Make a bold statement! The Color Brights story vividly reflects an eclectic mix of Eastern and Western cultures. The diverse elements are united by one thing: saturated color. This story has real life and luster, whether in the form of antique Christmas glass baubles, bundles of silk fabric and thread, or old mismatched buttons. The elements here are bold and graphic, from the flowers to the favors. This story has a touch of frivolity and fiesta to it . . . not for the shy and retiring bride!

The Color Brights story is light and bright. A light, airy backdrop makes the festive colors "pop" all the more. The homemade bunting is a mix of silk dupion and metallic chiffon, which gives it the wonderful dual effect of intense colors and floating translucence. The edges of the triangles were pinked to cut down on the amount of sewing. (You will need more than you think, so be generous with your measurements.) In order to jazz up these very simple wooden folding chairs, I attached strips of old colored-paper shelf edging.

A festive, flowing door curtain of crepe paper shimmies in the slightest breeze. (Be sure to keep it dry—crepe paper loses its dye and its fun the moment it comes in contact with water.) You could use either ribbons or strips of colored fabric—as with the bunting, play around with solid and translucent fabrics.

For an intriguing twist on the traditional floral display, large flower blooms have been submerged in water (right). To stop them from floating to the surface, some were anchored down with white pebbles.

Brightly-colored buttons prove suitably celebratory and a perfect complement to the Color Brights story. Alternatively, consider using beads, dried flowers, or an array of colorful ribbons.

These favors have an international flair! Italian amaretto biscuits were wrapped in brightly colored glassine paper with tasseled ends tied in a variety of ribbons. The date of the wedding was painted on with metallic copper paint. The glass jars filled with the favor cookies were adorned with copper hearts with the words "Eat Me," "Enjoy," and "With Love" etched into the surface with a craft knife. For other sweets with global appeal, consider Turkish delight, exotic imported candies, or fortune cookies with messages custom-scripted for the occasion.

A playful combination of contrasting materials and techniques, these napkin rings pull double duty as place cards—always a helpful approach if your tables are a little small or you want to keep them fairly uncluttered. The ribbon flowers were inspired by the dahlia table flowers and could be substituted with paper or brightly colored plastic ones. To introduce even more color, the napkins themselves could be mixed and matched. The napkin rings take their inspiration from the collage 'Trust in Your Heart' (at left), which is a riot of clashing colors united by one element—the heart.

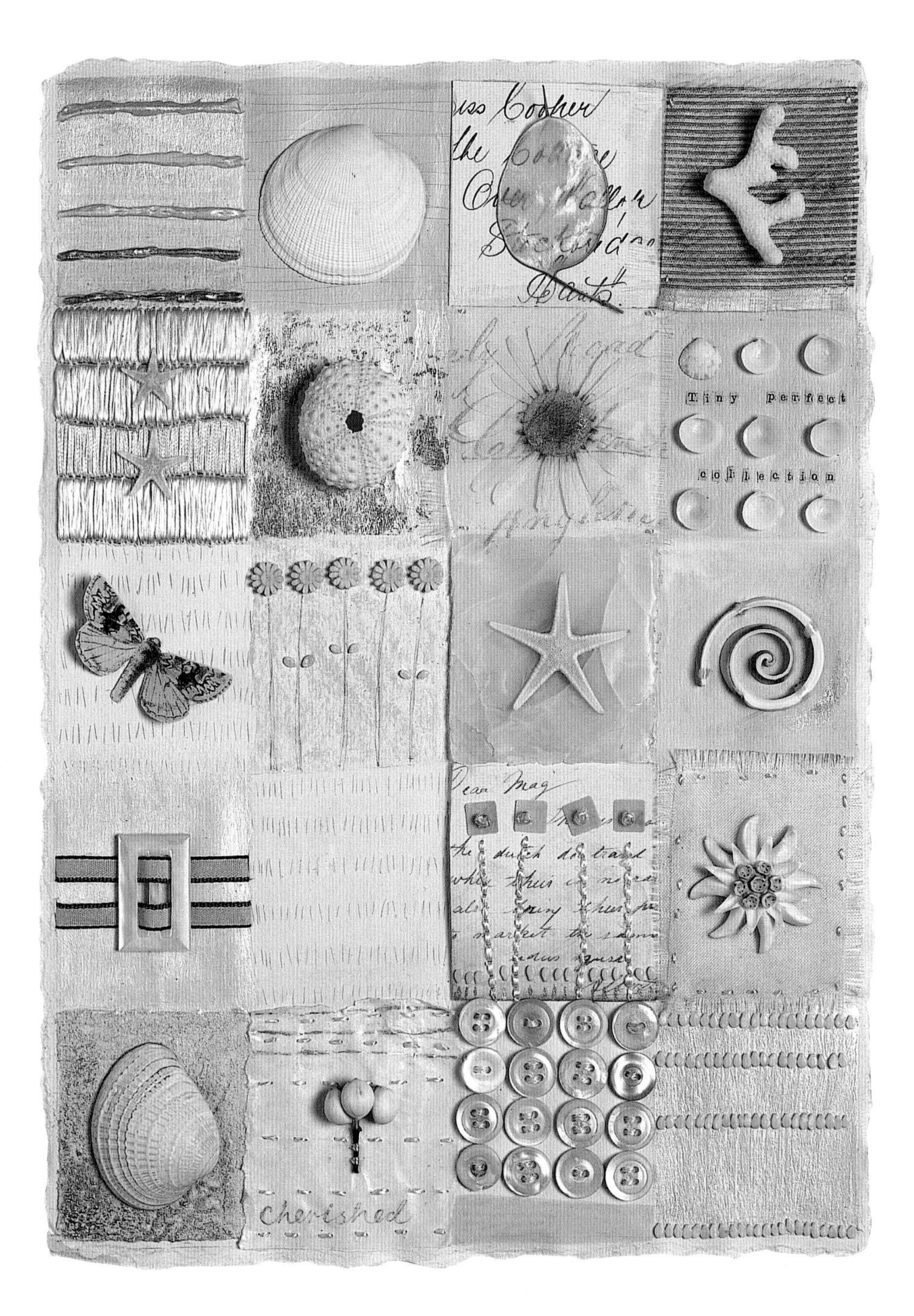
Tiny perfect
collection
Dear Mag
cherished

Antique Whites

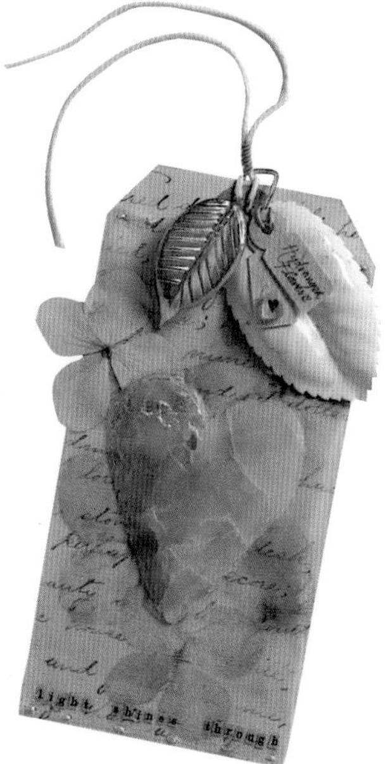

Crisp white tables and
frosty cake boxes, with
sparkler packs,
and a fluttering
welcome wreath.

ANTIQUE WHITES INSPIRATION

This visual theme was inspired by my collection of mother-of-pearl buttons, sea-washed chalk, and etched glass. I love the look of white-on-white and all the subtleties that are to be found within this color palette—the contrast of the flat, polished, pearly buttons against the smooth, undulating powdery surface of the sea-washed chalk, the frosted glass, and the translucent silk chiffon.

The Antique Whites story is in complete contrast to the multicultural and eclectic Color Brights theme. Antique Whites is inspired by times past and the faded memory of a bygone era. The color palette of whites and pearly creams is complemented with cool greys and warm Antique silvers, with touches of ice blue and sepia.

This more formal wedding is set in an elegantly traditional room with the fireplace as the focal point. The colors of this story are complemented by the decoration of the room with its pale blue walls and stone fireplace—a perfect setting for Antique Whites. As cozy as a fire can be, it can also be a little overpowering in a room full of people; so what would have been a fire is replaced with decorated cherry twigs bathed in a soft glow of light from fairy lights and candles. This is as charming and welcoming as a roaring fire.

The inspiration for these three boxes comes from far and wide. The large white box was inspired by the exquisite paper and ribbon that French patisseries use to wrap their *gateaux*. The other two boxes take their aesthetic inspiration from Japan, starting with handmade Japanese paper.

Everyone loves sparklers! The mix of stitched, handmade papers, gilded antique stars, and metallic threads allude to antique Indian saris. These delightful packages are a luminescent preview to the thrills to come.

This soft, fluttering feather wreath is perfectly complemented by a translucent silk chiffon ribbon. With its hint of ice blue trim and silver lettering, the gossamer ribbon catches the light as it wafts in the breeze.

Sea-washed chalk adorned with hand-painted hearts and pale blue and silver dragées spread messages of love across the wedding tables.

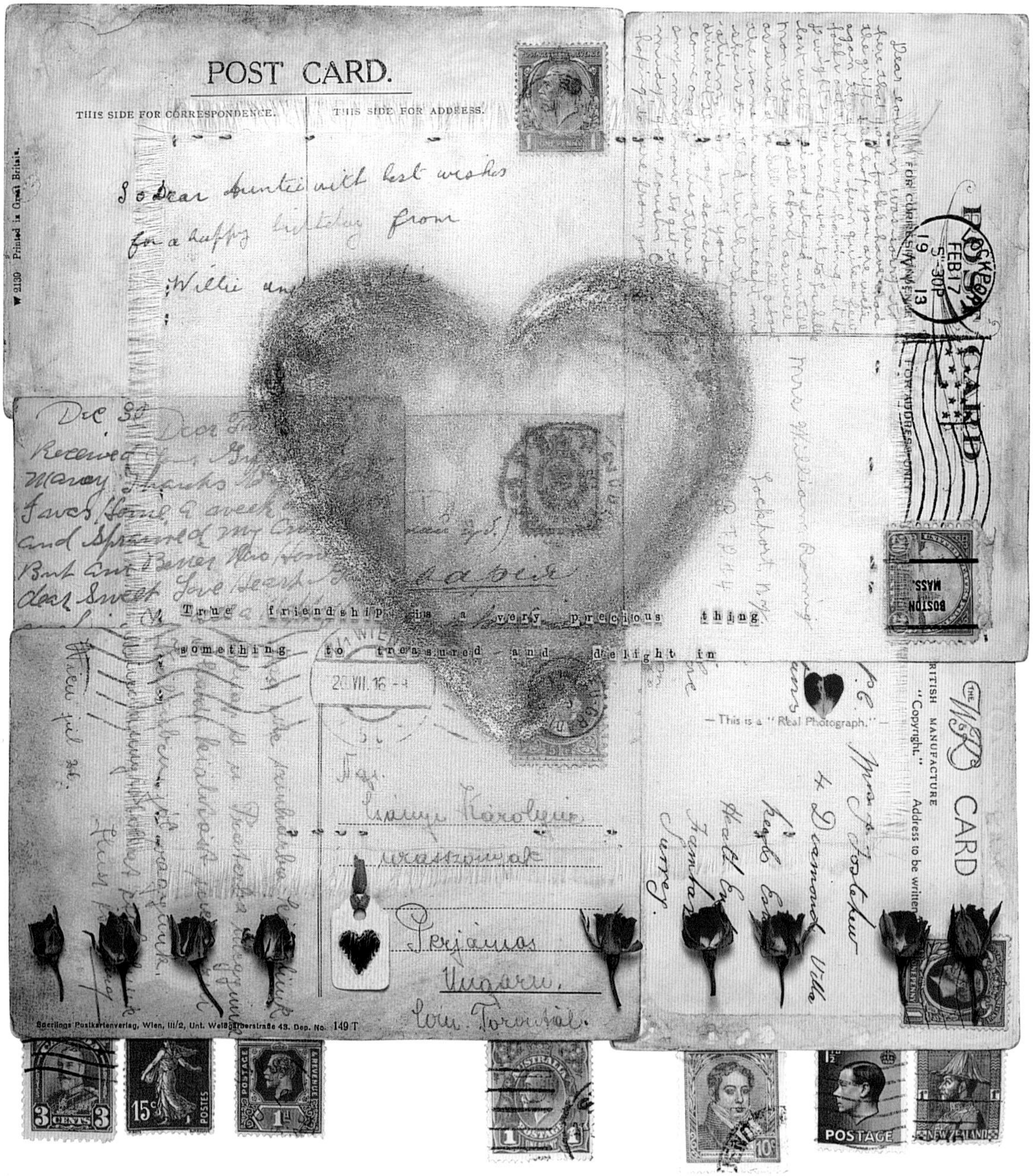

POST CARD.

THIS SIDE FOR CORRESPONDENCE. THIS SIDE FOR ADDRESS.

So Dear Auntie with best wishes for a happy birthday from Willie

W 2130 Printed in Great Britain.

True friendship is a very precious thing something to treasured and delight in

20.VII.16

LOCKPORT FEB 17 5-30P 19 13

POST CARD

FOR CORRESPONDENCE

FOR ADDRESS ONLY

BOSTON MASS.

— This is a "Real Photograph." —

BRITISH MANUFACTURE "Copyright." Address to be written

CARD

Sperlings Postkartenverlag, Wien, III/2, Unt. Weißgerberstraße 43. Dep. No. 149 T

3 CENTS 3

15c POSTES

POSTAGE 1d REVENUE

AUSTRALIA

10c

POSTAGE

NEW ZEALAND

Stationery

The joy of paper—envelopes,
invitations, menus, order
of service, place names, and
thank-you cards.

THE JOY OF PAPER

When choosing the paper for your wedding stationery you will discover a delightful array of textures, colors, weights, patterns, prints, and decorative edging. Let the paper inspire your design ideas for your entire wedding stationery collection including invitations, envelopes, order of service, menus, paper napkins and place names, cake boxes, and thank-yous. If the paper you've fallen for is unprintable, just tip on a standard printed page, concealing the glued joint with ribbon ties, tags, or *les objets trouvé.*

Take time out to browse in stationery stores for various ideas on envelopes, envelope enclosures, inks, seals, and stickers. For seals with a difference, use antique buttons with patterned surfaces to create delicious impressed designs on your envelopes. Stick the button onto the end of a pencil to save your fingers.

An envelope is a promise and preview of what's inside. Envelopes can be clean and simple or as extravagant and complex as you like. They can be textured, colored, embossed, and adorned. If we look to the past, we can see many techniques that lend a special flair and an air of elegance worthy of the occasion. Sealing wax, for instance, comes in many colors, and can be used not only as a sealer but also to attach adornments like a ribbon, or as shown, a pressed daisy. You might also consider stamping your initials, family crest, hearts, or love birds.

I wanted our invitations to be clean and simple, to have a personal feel, and, if at all possible, to have a tactile quality. The paper I chose had a crisp, clean look that I knew would serve as a nice neutral foundation for the various "attachments." The color also matched that of the mount board I use for all my artwork, so it seemed like a natural idea. The invitation was tied with hand-dyed silk ribbon that matched the color of the bridesmaid's dress, and hanging from this were three tags, one with a silk-stitched heart, and two color-washed tags with an embossed "S" for Sarah and "R" for Robert. I wrote the message on the inside of the card, in my own hand, then had it color-copied in a deep graphite color so it looked as if I had handwritten each invitation in pencil.

INSPIRATIONAL IMAGES AND DETAILS

Your invitations can be as simple or as complex as you like—from printed artwork to complex folds and ties. If you would like to include a color image within the design but need to keep costs down, consider color-copying your original image and gluing it on. Also, consider tactile additions to your image using pressed flowers, fabric and ribbons, buttons and beads, as well as old, printed imagery such as stamps, postcards, and labels.

Have you tucked away treasures, just waiting for the right occasion to use them? What better place than in your invitations. Create an image that is a unique celebration of your union by incorporating images and items that have special meaning to you and your partner.

Antique Whites: (upper left) A sublimely subtle color palette of creams and whites with touches of antique silver and cool pale blue give beautiful new life to the old expression, "something old, something new, something borrowed, something blue." Country Lanes: (upper right) Dried daisies and fresh green gingham ribbon are used to capture the essence of the English countryside in early summer. The two interlocking daisy rings symbolize the sentiment "two become one." Color Brights: (bottom) Bold colors and textile elements create a statement of passion and adventure. Faded antique postcards and stamps are complemented by bright satin ribbon.

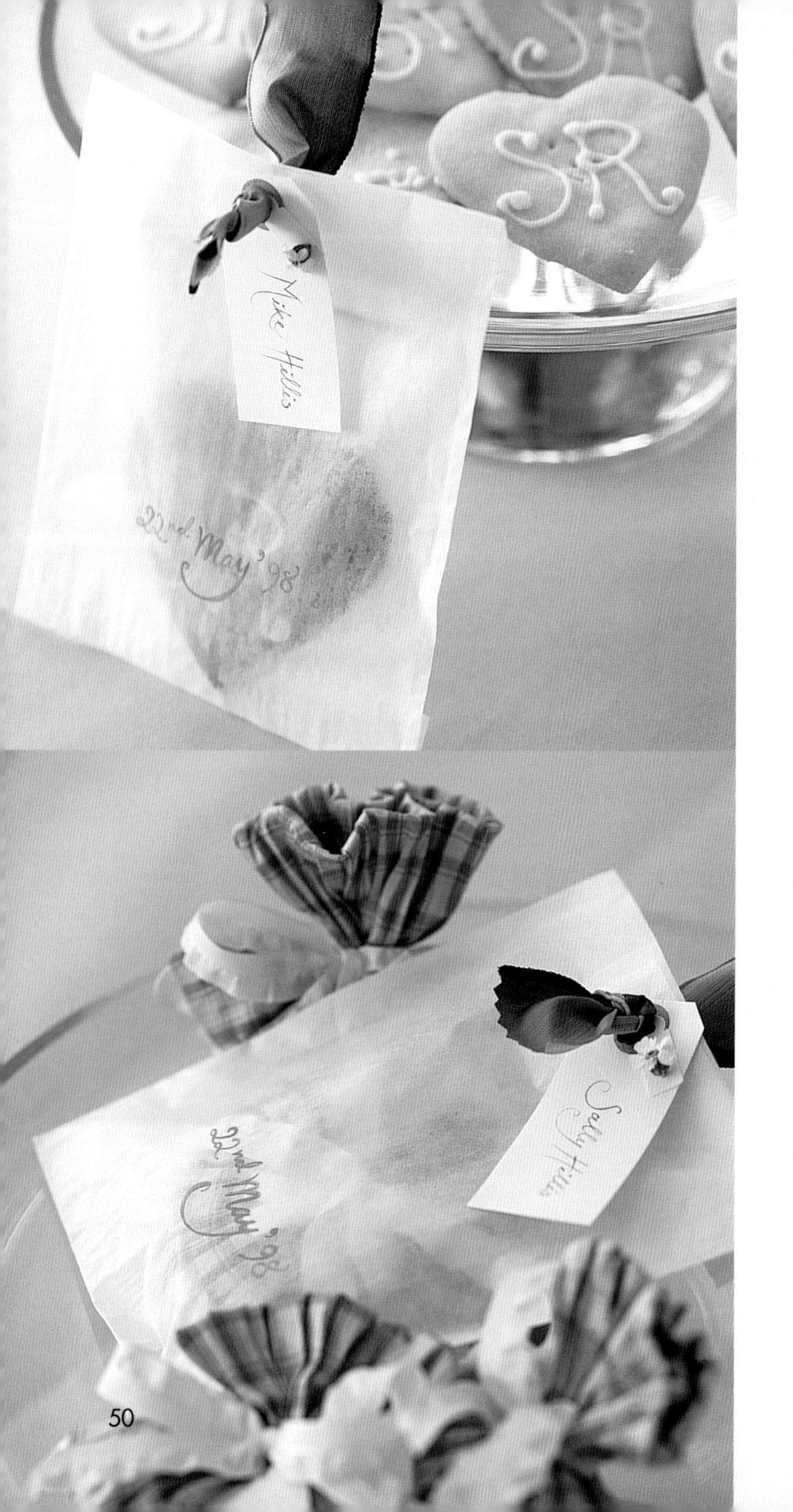

Our wedding place cards also doubled as wedding favors: lavender bags for the girls and homemade heart-shaped shortbread biscuits for the boys. I used glassine bags, which I then rubber-stamped with our wedding date in pale green paint. I had the rubber stamp made using my handwriting to tie in with all the other writing in the stationery. The tops of the bags were secured using a wide wire-edged ribbon. Attached to this was the guest's name written on a tag plus an even smaller tag with a dried daisy glued on. The lavender bag was made from the same fabric as that of the bridesmaid's dress, and had two tiny tags attached with embossed "s" and "r," while the heart-shaped shortbread biscuits had an iced "s" and "r."

By thinking beyond the restrictions of a traditional "card," you can create a place marker that doubles as a guest favor—especially handy when tabletop space is limited.

Tim Graham
Freddie Draper
Margo Tantau
Denise Fiedler

Inspired by the English garden, a medley of terra-cotta pots and wire baskets is planted with old metal plant labels bearing the guests' place names. The settings were a combination of junk shop finds and terra-cotta pots passed down from my grandfather and mother.

Three different thank-you cards echo and extend the essence of the ceremony. Consider using photographs from the big day in a montage with flowers, beads, or ribbons. Try photo-transferring an image onto the same fabric as used for your wedding dress or veil.

For our thank-you card to my parents, I used pressed daisies salvaged from the wedding arrangements. The message in cut-out letters carried special meaning as the letters were copied from one of my mother's poetry books she had when she was at school. It is a book of poems by Byron, and she gave it to me when we returned from a wonderful holiday together in northern Tuscany. We had been staying in the area where Keats, Shelley, and Byron had once lived, so the pages from this book were a perfect addition to the collection of treasures I brought back with me from that trip.

Mexican Daisies

Let the beauty of nature
inspire your
bouquets,
boutonnieres,
chair ties,
table flowers,
wreaths,
swags, and confetti cones.

OUR WEDDING FLOWERS

I adore flowers so trying to decide what to have at our wedding was (while still very pleasant) not the easiest of tasks. My two chief criteria were color palette and overall theme. As far as colors were concerned, I wanted whites and creams with just the palest of blushes of peach and apricot. To this, I wanted to add accents of soft mauve and a variety of greens—from pale fresh green through lime, to silver, with a touch of darkness being introduced with bronze. As for the overall impression, I wanted it to be informal but bountiful—a bit like the way I garden. I hate to see bare earth, so my flower beds are always jam-packed with plants. I like to use plants that appeal to me—I am not led by fashion. For example, I like to mix what some people consider weeds with cultivated plants. An often-overlooked element to consider with flowers is scent. At our wedding, three perfumes pervaded the arrangements: lily, rose, and honeysuckle.

Our wedding flowers were a mixture of wild, homegrown, and market-bought. The wild ones were from the hedgerows that have always inspired me with their humble bounty of dog rose, white campion, stitchwort, and cowparsley. To me, these white campions always looked like stars dancing in a sea of lush green. As far as I'm concerned you have to go a long way to beat quiet country lanes filled with cowparsley wafting in the dappled sunlight of late spring. The homegrown flowers were the old-fashioned English roses—Madame Alfred du Carrie, Alberic Barrie, and Wheatwood. Also, most of the foliage used came from either my mother's garden or from the gardens of her friends, who were all amazingly willing to strip prized specimens for the occasion. The foliage was a mixture of silver and bronze with a touch of lime. This included some of my all-time favorites—bronze fennel, alchemilla mollis, and a broad-leafed sage. The flowers from the market were peonies, lilies, September daisies, ranunculus, and white and mauve delphiniums, along with many more.

The flowers on the tables were arranged in beautiful cream-ware pots made by a friend. In celebration of the occasion, we had our names and the date stamped into the pots—very regal. As one friend pointed out, they looked a bit like royal coronation jugs! What was so nice about this was that I was able to give the pots away after the wedding to family members and close friends. A simple alternative to having pots custom made would be to personalize existing pots with paint and stencil.

At the entrance to the reception, I had a huge antique stone urn filled with wild daisies, white campion, and a mixture of wonderful grasses. The juxtaposition of this formal, classical pot overflowing in an unmanageable riot of humble flowers looked wonderful and very striking.

Boutonnieres normally consist of a single bloom or a sprig of foliage and sometimes get a bit overlooked. You can create an interesting boutonniere with just a little care and attention. Make sure they are securely fastened, and don't forget to give someone extra pins to hand out in case there aren't enough to go around. Also, if you are using a scented bloom, check to assure that none of your bridal party suffers from hay fever.

If you do not have a specific theme or color palette for your wedding, consider starting with your favorite flower or fabric and building from there.

If you are as mad as I am and are considering arranging your own flowers, I offer these pointers:
a) Take up any offers of help—as you will need it—whether it be gathering all the flowers and foliage, preparing them, or arranging them.
b) Make sure you have enough buckets and enough cool space to store the precious cargo, particularly if the weather is hotting up.
c) Make sure your containers are waterproof; if not, seal them well before use.
d) It would be good to have a little "play around" with the table arrangements before you start your production line.
e) Make sure you have a good pair of garden shears; otherwise you will be going nuts by the end of the day—which is not a good state for the bride to be in on the eve of her big day.

COUNTRY LANES

These flowers reflect the English hedgerows in early summer when they are a sea of nodding daisies wafting in amongst waves of grass.

A variety of cultivated daisies are used to create the contrast in scale found in the wild. These are mixed with one huge clover, wild and cultivated grasses, bronze fennel, and golden marjoram. BOUQUET: The flowers were simply tied with a large pale green-and-cream gingham silk ribbon. The flower girl's posies were attached to the backs of the chairs at the head table. Again, these little country posies were tied with gingham ribbon. BOUTONNIERES: The daisy was my starting point; but again, we added interest by playing with scale and composition. The third boutonniere was a charming posy of antique paper flowers arranged like a miniature version of the bride's bouquet. Tied with a cotton-covered wire, it enabled us to secure and position the tie exactly as we liked.

Be bold! Dahlias have intense colors and quite striking graphic shapes, and have been considered a little old-fashioned until recently—but their time is coming again. Deep burgundy-red roses and velvety cockscombs echo the richness of the silk ribbon and dupion bunting.

COLOR BRIGHTS

BOUQUET: A fabulously bright collection—the flowers are surrounded by a ring of ribbons and a huge, color-saturated silk ribbon bow. The ribbons, like the flowers, unapologetically both clash with and complement each other. Stems are wrapped with moss-green rat-tail cord. BOUTONNIERES: These echo the bouquets with their jewel-like clashing colors and textile qualities. The rose petals and ruffles of the cockscomb give the luxurious impression of silk velvet. The deep-red rose boutonniere has bright orange glass-flower beads tucked in amongst its petals, adding to its richness. Shiny copper-wire binding is the finishing touch.

A tight bouquet of Old English garden roses is offset by its collar of wrapped silk thread and mother-of-pearl buttons.

ANTIQUE WHITES

These flowers have the same softness and subtleties to be found elsewhere in this story. Whites, creams, grays, and pearly silvers were the starting point with soft, feathery, translucent, and opaque qualities. You will be surprised at the complexity of colors to be found within a white and cream palette.

BOUQUET (right): The beautiful feather-like blooms of the peony are complemented by the lacy flower heads of the climbing hydrangea.

BOUTONNIERES: The boutonnieres reflect the reserved nature of this story with singular blooms or seed pods accompanied by antique silver ribbon or pearly glass leaves. The snowberries boutonniere (second from left) even includes a message of love inscribed on the opaque pod of the honesty seed.

SEASONAL FLOWERS

SPRING
ALMOND FLOWER Hope
AMARYLLIS Splendid beauty
ANEMONE Forsaken
BLUEBELL Everlasting love
DAFFODIL Regard
DAISY Innocence
FORGET-ME-NOT True love, Forget-me-not
HYACINTH Playfulness
JONQUIL Affection returned
LEMON BLOSSOM Fidelity in love
LILAC First love
LILY OF THE VALLEY Happiness
MIMOSA Sensitiveness
SNOWDROP Hope
VIOLET Faithfulness

SUMMER
DAMASK ROSE Brilliant complexion, Freshness
FOUR-LEAFED CLOVER Be mine
HIBISCUS Delicate beauty
HOLLYHOCK Ambition
HONEYSUCKLE Devoted affection
PEONIES Bashfulness
PINK CARNATION Woman in love
ROSE Romance
SWEET PEA Everlasting pleasure
TUBEROSE Voluptuousness
WHITE CLOVER Think of me
WHITE LILY Purity, Modesty
WHITE ROSE I am worthy of you

AUTUMN
AMARANTH COCKSCOMB Affection
EVERLASTING PEA Lasting pleasure
FENNEL Worthy of all praise, Strength
HONESTY Honesty, Fascination
OLIVE Peace I am worthy of you
RED CHRYSANTHEMUM I love you
ROSEMARY Remembrance
SAGE Esteem, Wisdom

WINTER
AMARANTH GLOBE Unfading love
CAMELLIA Perfect loveliness
CAPE JASMINE I am too happy
GLORY FLOWER Glorious beauty
HELIOTROPE Devotion, Faithfulness
HONEY FLOWER Love sweet and secret
IVY Fidelity
MYRTLE Love
ORANGE BLOSSOM Bridal festivities
ORCHID Beauty
SWEET ALYSSUM Worth, Beyond beauty
VENETIAN MALLOW Delicate beauty
WHITE DITTANY OF CRETE Passion

TABLE FLOWERS

When choosing your table flowers, don't forget to consider the height of the arrangement. You want your guests to be able to chat freely without having to peer over towering floral creations.

COUNTRY LANES: A wonderful, antique, French storage jar perfectly reflects the simplicity of the overall theme and complements the humble country arrangement.

COLOR BRIGHTS: Table flowers are arranged in a collection of mismatched drinking glasses. Even though the containers are a mixture of sizes, their shapes are uniformly clean and simple.

ANTIQUE WHITES: Looking more like delicate feathers than flowers, three huge white hydrangeas nestle into large clam shells, whose scalloped edges echo those of the flowers' petals. A blue-and-white chiffon ribbon, with the bride's and groom's names written in silver, adds a splash of color.

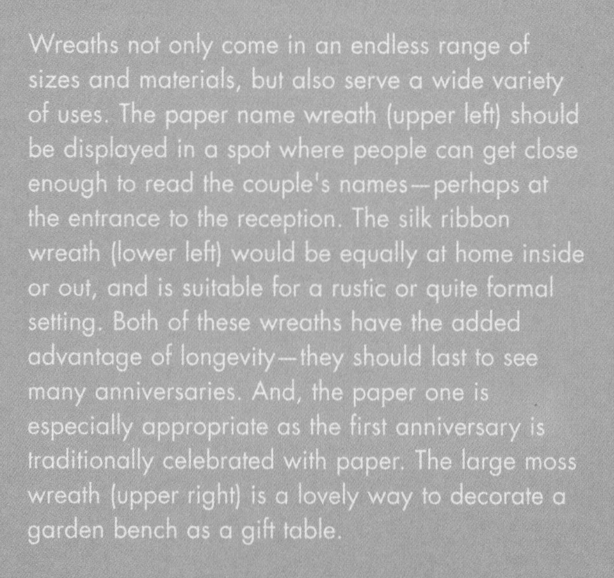

Wreaths not only come in an endless range of sizes and materials, but also serve a wide variety of uses. The paper name wreath (upper left) should be displayed in a spot where people can get close enough to read the couple's names—perhaps at the entrance to the reception. The silk ribbon wreath (lower left) would be equally at home inside or out, and is suitable for a rustic or quite formal setting. Both of these wreaths have the added advantage of longevity—they should last to see many anniversaries. And, the paper one is especially appropriate as the first anniversary is traditionally celebrated with paper. The large moss wreath (upper right) is a lovely way to decorate a garden bench as a gift table.

This elegant staircase is decorated with swags of white and ice-blue silk-chiffon. Sunlight streams through handmade translucent paper cones filled with white hydrangea blossoms that punctuate the swags.

Roman newlyweds were showered with almonds, symbolic of fertility. Later vogue was for rice, and now paper confetti. Pictured are three confetti mixtures.

LOVE'S love knows not how to chide

Candles

Create a romantic atmosphere with
storm lanterns,
tea lights,
tree lights,
and fairy lights.

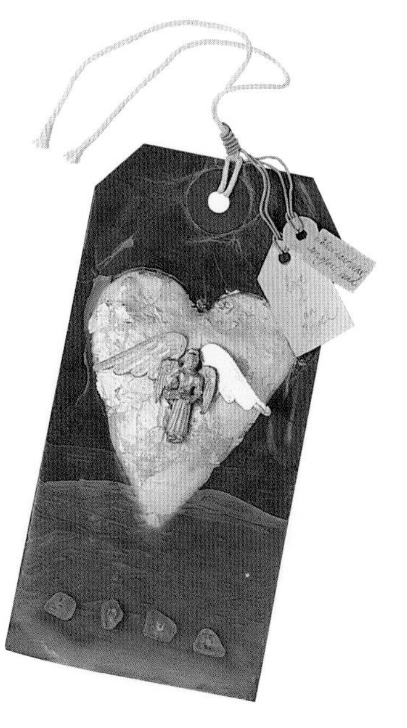

Candles are a firm favorite of mine. They create such a different atmosphere–a softness that is missing from an electric light; a touch of romance and nostalgia.

French yogurt jars find luminous new life as hanging lanterns in the verdant orchard setting of the Country Lanes wedding. The lanterns are attached to the limbs by wire that has been wrapped around the jars' lips. Delicate twists and twirls at the ends of the wires add a dash of whimsy. Make the wires longer than you think you'll need, in case you need to twist a wire around a twig rather than just hang it.

Fireplaces can be a bit of a conundrum if they are not lit with fires or filled with huge floral arrangements. Here, a large glass vase is nestled in amongst sea-washed chalk, shells, feathers, and white votives. The cherry tree twigs are adorned with silver letters, a silver floral garland, and delicate fairy lights.

On the mantelpiece, soft light emanating from a antique Christmas tree topper illuminates a collection of clear glass vases filled with giant clematis and hydrangea blooms.

Winter grass, Sea shell and pebble, Scrabble letters, Birch bark, Sea shells, Pebble and rosebud, Pussy willow twigs, silk thread, Vintage postcard and Wax, Sweet wrapper and Summer garlic skin.

Favors

Present your guests with
packages,
parcels,
and purses.

Vintage moss-filled seed trays make the perfect favor for the Country Lanes wedding party. The trays were personalized with the couples' names and an appropriate sentiment for the day. The tags were decorated with old seed packets, huge pale green seeds, seed pods, and daisies in various forms.

Use small details from your wedding story to add flair and fun to this delightful collection of wooden boxes. Filled with a selection of your favorite flower seeds, shells, sweet-scented soaps, potpourri, chocolates, or a delicious medley of dried or candied fruits, the boxes become wedding favors sure to be universally appreciated.

Favors can be as simple and humble, as you like. The beeswax candles are tied together with frayed ice blue chiffon with a narrow printed paper middle—simple but very striking. The drawstring chiffon bag contains sea-washed chalk with a painted heart. Alternatively, you could paint on the wedding date or a single word that ties in to the message rubber-stamped on the drawstring ribbon.

These delightful little 3" felt bags are a gift in themselves, but could contain a variety of wonderful surprises . . . dragées, chocolates, a favorite poem, sea shells, a packet of seeds, painted pebbles, or any other treasure particularly suited to your wedding theme.

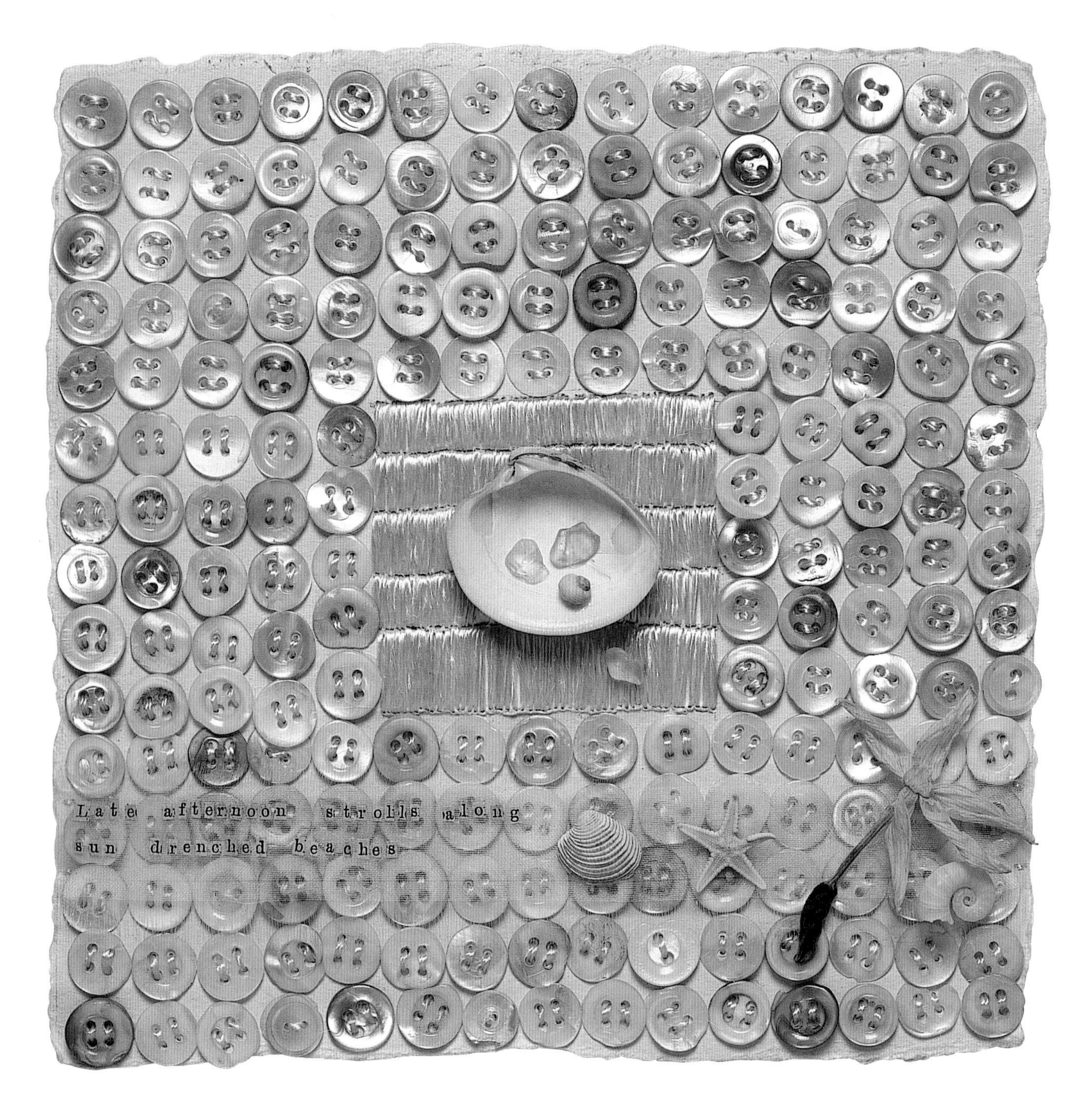
Late afternoon strolls along
sun drenched beaches

Bridal Party Accessories

Delightful finery for brides and
flower girls,
shawls,
shoes,
wreaths,
wings, and ring pillows.

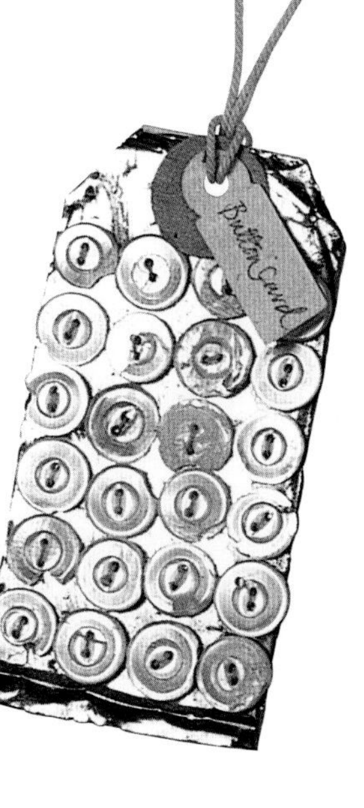

My accessories were very simple, small, and detailed, as I did not want to distract from my dress. For my hair, I had two antique silk flowers. My bag, which belonged to my grandmother, was adorned with a flower that matched those in my hair. The pearly beaded "S" and "R," which hung down from my bouquet, complemented the beading on my dress.

A simple but sweet gift for a bride is the "message bottle" filled with antique good luck charms, messages of hope and happiness, and, of course, elements tying in with the old saying, "something old, something new, something borrowed, something blue." My jewelry—including earrings made of freshwater pearl clusters and pale blue aquamarine beads—was made especially for the occasion by a friend who is a jeweler.

Handmade from exquisite fabrics and trims, these beautiful shawls are a joy to behold and to wear. The Country Lanes shawl is made from a soft spring-green silk chiffon with an embroidered pattern of leaves and daisies. The ends of the shawl are finished off with pom-poms made from gathered silk ribbon. The Color Brights wrap is made from pieced silk satin, edged with beaded trim and finished off with a large single silk flower.

The Antique Whites shawl is fashioned from an ethereal floating chiffon with white-on-white embroidering. The edging has the thinnest sliver of pale blue silk ribbon, which in turn has been edged with pale cream velvet ribbon with a scalloped edge and a die-cut pattern within the velvet ribbon.

Have fun with your flower girls' shoes! These satin shoes will bring a smile to any girl's face and provide the finishing touch to darling little princess outfits!

This Color Brights ribbon wreath is an appropriately high-spirited match for the little girl bouncing down the aisle. Originally inspired by a jumble of ribbons in the ribbon box, the wreath is fashioned from short strips of ribbon in a variety of sizes and colors.

Flower girl outfits offer a perfect opportunity to introduce some whimsy into your wedding. Have fun with their outfits! Add a little angelic frivolity, and they will look all the more adorable.

These pillows were inspired by antique pincushions that were very ornate and a work of art in themselves. The elements that make up the pillows are taken from the wedding saying, "something old, something new, something borrowed, something blue"–the new element being the wedding bands. Both of the pillows are filled with lavender and would serve as a lovely daily reminder of your wedding if nestled amongst the pillows on your bed. This forget-me-not ring box is also to be treasured–and is, I think, a pretty charming way of reminding the best man about his duties! If you would like to use pressed flowers when out of season, remember to press them when they are in flower.

Intertwined daisies and bound-together wedding bands nestle on a velvety cushion of lush moss.

Postcard and felt leaf, Pineapple leaf and button, ribbon and stamp
Seashells, map, sea glass, button, leaf and rose bud, postcard and
Sea urchin, vintage fabric and sea glass, sea shell, silk thread 'G'
and vintage button card.

Gifts

Thoughtful thank-yous from grateful couples,
gift tags and wrapping,
engraved hearts,
gift boxes,
and flower girl thank-yous.

For my parents' thank-you gift, I found two old terra-cotta pots with which I was delighted, as both of my parents–but particularly my mother—adored their garden. I found these several months before the wedding as I didn't want to leave such an important thing until the last minute. I planted them well in advance, and kept them a secret until the big day. When I heard shrieks of delight from the garden, I knew that they had discovered them while taking an early morning stroll before the madness and jollity of the day began.

The tags in the pots come in the form of two silver-winged messengers bringing love and thanks. In keeping with the natural setting of this gift, the birds are attached to twig supports planted in with the flowers.

For our wedding thank-yous, gentlemen were given antique bottles of port and ladies received silver cast-flower earrings.

When your guests have gone to the trouble and expense of saving a day for you in their busy lives, perhaps shopping for something special to wear–or in the least having their apparel cleaned and pressed–making a trip to the hair or nail salon, shopping for your wedding gift, and traveling to be there on time, it's a lovely gesture to present them each with a special gift as a memento of your wedding day.

Follow your theme idea and wedding colors in matters of gift presentation. If you used tissues, parchment, ribbons, herbs, buds, or blossoms, complete the overall appearance of the gift or wedding reception tables by keeping your guest gifts in harmony with all of the other decorative details you've chosen.

The wire-edged variegated green ribbon in a subtle "nature" shade used to tie the men's and ladies' gifts (at left) has been gently crimped to hold a sculptural form. Its three-dimensional quality is in harmony with the twig of white berries tucked beneath each knot.

There are many ways to say thank-you, but few could be more beautiful or elegant than this etched silver heart with its simple message of gratitude and affection.

The silver fruit boxes are beautiful gifts in themselves; but in this case, I have used them as a richly decorative box for jewelry. The tissue-paper wrapping of the silver fruit was inspired by the wrapping found on fresh fruit at the market.

The cufflink box was decorated with heart-shaped seedpods and pale green ribbon. The inside of the box was lined with dark green moss that provided a perfect cushion for the engraved silver cufflinks. Hearts have always been a favorite of mine, and in this case, a wonderful way to express heartfelt thanks.

The etched heart was originally a Christmas ornament that I sprayed with a product that gives an instant effect of etched glass. The silver heart was engraved by a jeweler—one side reading "Thank you," and the other, "Love is a precious thing." You might also consider any number of significant messages such as the dates of your wedding, a line from your favorite poem or song, names or initials, or another message of love, thanks, or gratitude.

For my flower girl, I commissioned one of my mother's very talented friends to make a doll. This exquisite creation was a huge hit with Laura. I had asked if the doll could be dressed in a mini version of Laura's dress and head piece. The amazing thing was that not only did the dress beautifully match Laura's, but the doll itself looked like a miniature Laura.

Other gift ideas for young ones are engraved silver bracelets or silver napkin rings as a souvenir of the event, or possibly a collector's edition of a favorite author like Beatrix Potter or A. A. Milne.

Vintage photographic card, compass and copper star, Victorian silk button and sea shells. Silk thread stitched letter, Old ticking, shell fragment and bone domino, Old post card and Tulip leaf skeleton, a face from the past and Star collection, Starfish and Guinea fowl feathers, Mrs. Thompson on her way to France, and Vintage metal thread and button, Beach comber collection and ornamental leaves, Seawashed shell and china, ridged shell. Old ruler, snowberries and Turitella shell section, Key and buttons, Mussel shell.

Photography

Capture those magical memories in
photo albums,
brag books,
picture frames, and
keepsake boxes.

PHOTOGRAPHS
C
Tom and Lucy

My wedding photo album was a gift from my godfather. This beautiful leather-bound book with embossed leaves is the perfect album for me. I personalized it by adding the vintage silk ribbon and the copper tag with our names embossed. The pressed daisy was from our wedding flowers.

Whatever style or size you select for your wedding photo album, be certain that you are not only comfortable with it but pleased enough with it to share it for years to come with friends and loved ones in your home.

This is a perfect gift for parents and in-laws, or a perfect keepsake just for you. It saves you having to carry around a huge selection of photos from your wedding, and it spares unsuspecting victims from having to relive your ceremony in excruciating detail. (For some reason, one's wedding photos are not as absorbing to other people as they will be to you—funny that!) The books shown here tie in with the Country Lanes and the Antique White stories highlighted throughout this book. For a purse or pocket-sized album, you could make a simple slip cover for an easily obtained plastic mini-album.

A celebration photo of your day finds a perfect match in this festive frame. I took all the elements from the napkin rings and married them together to create this jewel-like vignette.

I made this frame for my parents and gave it to them for the first Christmas following our wedding. I chose the preserved daisies as they were quite a prominent feature at our wedding. You could alternatively use pressed flowers, confetti, or details left over from the making of your dress such as buttons, ribbons, and lace.

An artful reference to the tiny pearl buttons on my wedding dress, this button-heart picture frame was created from my collection of vintage mother-of-pearl buttons. This was our thank-you to my parents for all their love and their huge effort in giving me away in such a special manner.

You will probably have kept many treasures from the preparations of your wedding as well as from the actual day itself. A box specifically designed to hold all these treasures will prevent the gradual dispersal of all those well-loved elements over the years. In my keepsake box, I have scraps of fabric from my dress and the dresses of my bridesmaids, a piece of satin-covered cord that my mother so patiently handstitched for the edging of my dress and train, covered buttons, the order of service and wedding favors, the wire napkin rings my girlfriend so patiently made with dried rosemary, and a couple of champagne corks.

Gros-Grain Français
Pattern BEAUVAIS
10 Yards
Made in France

HOW TO MAKE IT

Step-by-step instructions for beautiful makes to enhance your wedding day.

Napkin Rings

page 19

Button Daisy

Supplies

• tissue paper (10" x 4½") • mother-of-pearl button • narrow green ribbon (9") • clear tape • craft glue • very fine scissors • fat pencil

Fold your tissue paper in half lengthwise to make a long narrow band, which you then loosely roll around a fat pencil. Make certain to keep both ends level. Slide the tube off the pencil. Keep in a roll by holding the end of the folded edge. Make cuts 1" deep down toward the folded edge, using very fine scissors. Try to make the fringe as fine as possible.

Once fringed, pinch the base and secure with clear tape. Then bend out the fringing/petals to open up the flower. Take a large vintage mother-of-pearl button and stitch or glue to the very center of the flattened flower.

Tie and knot your chosen "stalk" ribbon into a loop, leaving one end approximately 3" long. Then, glue the knot to the center of the back of your flower. ■

Ribbon Knot

Supplies

• wire-edged ribbon (12" length) • small metal daisy buttons • craft glue

This simple twist of ribbon has the detail at the ends with the metal daisy buttons.

Use a wire-edged ribbon to give the napkin tie structure. Glue metal daisies to the ends of the ribbon. ■

Metal Ring

Supplies

• silver wire • cardboard tube (2" diameter) • fresh herbs, like rosemary or thyme • wire cutters

This is what I used at my wedding. My girlfriend Margo made 110 of these, bless her!

Here we used about 34" of wire per napkin ring. Wrap the wire around a stiff cardboard tube.

Take both ends of the wire and twist around your rings in a decorative knot. This is to hold the wire together as well as to add detail to your design.

We tucked a small sprig of fresh herbs into each napkin. You can vary the herbs, but use varieties that don't wilt easily. Rosemary is shown, or thyme or bay is good. ■

Card Ring

Supplies

• greeting cards • desired embellishments • cardstock • craft glue • spray mount

Here I have photocopied a section of one of my paintings. To create something similar, greeting cards work quite nicely.

Cut 2" strips from the cards and paste together to create an image at least 8" long. Or, photocopy an image from your own artwork.

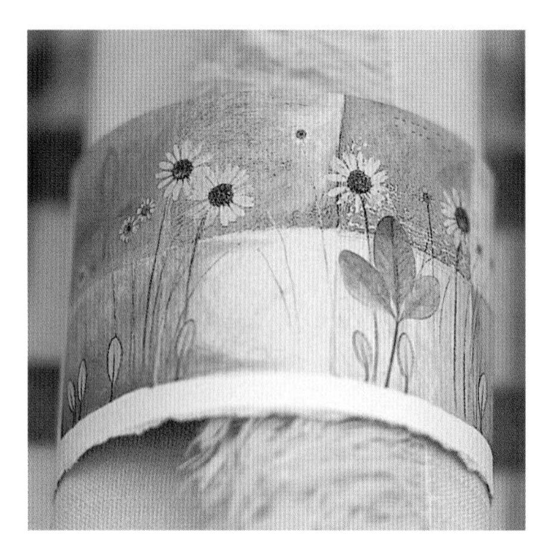

Color-copy your image onto uncoated art paper suitable for printing. This will make your photocopied image less shiny.

Spray-mount your color-copy onto cardstock to add structure to the napkin ring.

If you have the time or patience, glue on objects such as flowers, buttons, beads, or ribbons to add a little tactile quality to your napkin rings.

For these napkin rings, I added small pressed daisies. ■

Wrapped Saplings

page 20

First, choose your saplings, as these will dictate the size of the wrapping. Then, make a tube of cardstock to wrap around the sapling. This will give your package strength and protect the paper wrappings from moisture stains. Now they are ready to be wrapped.

Map Tag Sapling

Supplies

• sapling • cardstock • unbleached greaseproof paper (15" x 12") • old maps • moss-green frayed-edged ribbon or old cord • tags • green raffia • desired embellishments • pressed leaves • clear tape • craft glue

For these saplings, I used unbleached greaseproof paper. I wrapped the paper around the cardstock tube, tucking and taping it at the base. I also taped the side seam. Use this wrapping seam at the back so that there are no unsightly seams.

The package is tied at the top with some old wrapped cord I found in a junk shop in France. Have a look around your ribbon stores as a lot of the frayed-edged ribbons in the moss green colors look very organic and would easily capture this feel.

For the tag, which is attached with green raffia, I used an old ordnance survey map. Just glue your tag to the back of the map and cut out tag.

The decoration is an old carved-bone flower (a flea market find) with two pressed leaves tucked in. The last addition to this is the name tag. ■

Fern Tag Sapling

Supplies

• sapling • cardstock • unbleached greaseproof paper (15" x 12") • old postcards • pressed fern • paper butterfly • tags • clear tape • craft glue • spray mount

With the unbleached greaseproof paper, I crumpled it and smoothed it out flat before wrapping it around the sapling tube. This adds a nice contrasting surface to the package.

Wrap the tube as in the Map Tag Sapling shown on the left.

For the tag, I cut out an old postcard and decorated it with a pressed fern and paper butterfly. Attach the fern with spray mount. The butterfly is a photocopy of an old etched image. I then gave the butterfly a wash of watercolor. ■

Stitched-leaf Tag Sapling

Supplies

• sapling • cardstock • old maps • tags • green silk thread • clear tape

For the wrapping this time, I used an old map of the area. You can pick these up at tag sales, charity shops, and flea markets quite easily.

For the tag, this is a labor of love and I wouldn't recommend it to anyone! However, if you insist, draw out your desired design, in this case a lucky four-leafed clover. Carefully hand-stitch with a silk thread. This gives you a nice contrast between the glossy thread and the matte paper. ■

Daisy Tag Sapling

Supplies

• sapling • cardstock • unbleached greaseproof paper • old maps and postcards • pressed daisies • tags • green raffia • clear tape • craft glue

Here, I have combined the two wrapping materials, the unbleached greaseproof paper, and the old map. Cut a strip from the map 2" high and as long as you need to wrap around your sapling tube. Attach this to the top of the tube. Then wrap the greaseproof paper around the tube.

For the tag, again I cut up a color-copy of an old postcard. This time I used one with a pale green background, as I wanted the daisies to stand out. If you can't find postcards with a suitable colored background, just give the plain ones a wash of watercolor in your color of choice.

To save time, you could make a set of three or four images and then color-copy them. I glued on two types of daisies here, a lawn daisy and a Margarite.

The tags are attached to the saplings with green raffia. ■

Decorations
page 26–29

Window Dressing
Supplies

• length of cord to fit across window or door opening • a colorful variety of ribbons or crepe paper • decorative tacks or nails

Stretch the cord across the opening about 1" down from the top and secure each end of the cord with a decorative tack.

Measure the height of the opening and double this, plus an extra 4". (This is because you will be looping the ribbons around the cord that is stretched across the opening.)

Cut your ribbons to the desired lengths. Find the middle of a ribbon and loop over the cord to attach, threading the two ends through the loop. Repeat until the cord is covered. ■

Table Numbers
Supplies

• heavy white cardstock • bright acrylic paints • assorted buttons • instant-bond glue • wooden dowels

Cut out your numbers from heavy cardstock and paint the back of the numbers an appropriately bright color. In this case, I used Chinese red.

Select your buttons and arrange on top of the number. Glue in place.

Mount your numbers on wooden dowels that you have decorated with crepe paper, ribbons, and paints. ■

Favors
page 30

Amaretto Biscuits
Supplies

• wrapped amaretto biscuits • brightly colored glassine paper • assorted ribbons • metallic copper paint • craft knife

These biscuit wrappers are made from brightly colored glassine paper. The tasseled ends are tied up with a variety of ribbons. The date of the wedding is painted on in metallic copper paint.

To make these favors, use the wrapper from your amaretto biscuits as a template for your favor wrapper. Cut the wrappers from the glassine paper, adding ½" at the top and bottom. Stack your wrappers and, using a craft knife, make fine cuts about 1" deep to create your fringe.

On a separate piece of paper, work out exactly where you want the date to appear on the wrapper once your biscuit is wrapped. Then, trace the date onto each wrapper and go over it with metallic copper paint. To save time, you could rubber stamp the date onto each wrapper. ■

Napkin Rings Place Cards

page 31

Flowers

Supplies

• assorted ribbons • old buttons • green pipe cleaners or thick wire • florist tape • metallic copper paint • fabric and craft glues • wire cutters

The flowers are made using old buttons as the centers. Loop colorful ribbons and glue to the back of the button centers.

For the stems of the flowers, use either green pipe cleaners or thick wire. Cut twice the length you need for the stem of the flower. Fold it in half, thread the button onto the wire, and twist to secure it in the middle. Then, wrap the stems with florist tape.

Tie a length of wire-edged ribbon around the flower stem. With metallic copper paint, write a name or message onto the ribbon. ■

Copper Heart Napkin Ring

Supplies

• crepe paper • various widths of ribbon • rickrack • copper metal sheeting • old printed matter • pinking shears • double-sided tape • glue

The napkin rings are collaged papers, cut metal, fabrics, and silk thread.

Using pinking shears, cut a strip of crepe paper 7" long x 1¼" wide. Layer the varying widths of ribbons across the center of the crepe-paper band, using rickrack as your last layer. Double-sided tape works great for the layering process.

Cut out a 1" heart motif from a copper metal sheet. Attach to the middle of the band with double-sided tape.

Cut out letters from the old printed matter to spell the word "cherish," and glue the letters onto the band. ■

Fringed Napkin Ring

Supplies

• photocopy of old letter • crepe paper • copper metal sheet • silk thread • double-sided tape • craft glue • pinking shears • very fine scissors

Photocopy an old letter onto cream textured paper. Cut a strip 7" x 2". Stitch a heart onto the center of the paper band using silk thread.

With pinking shears, cut a 7" x 3" strip from a copper metal sheet. Tape the paper band to the copper band.

For the fringe, cut a strip of crepe paper 7" long x 1" wide. Roll the crepe paper into a tube and hold at the top. With fine scissors, make tiny cuts about ½" into the paper. Make your cuts as fine as possible. Unroll the paper and attach to the top and bottom of the copper band with double-sided tape.

Glue the two ends of the napkin ring together. ■

Collage Napkin Ring

Supplies

• photocopy of old letter • watercolor paint • silk thread • silk fabric scrap • seed beads • ribbon scraps • crepe paper • pinking shears • glue

Cut a 7" x 1½" strip from the same photocopy used for the Fringed Napkin Ring. Lightly sketch out your design onto the strip.

Add a light wash of color to the center square. When the paper is completely dried, stitch the heart design with silk thread.

The frayed square of silk fabric to the left of the heart is attached with a single stitch in each corner. The beads are then stitched or glued on.

To the right of the heart, I have layered and glued strips of ribbon and pinked crepe paper into different color combinations. ■

Cake Boxes

page 38

For all three boxes, I used purchased cake boxes in assorted sizes.

Embossed Box

Supplies

• cake box • embossed wallpaper • cream paper • pale blue watercolor paint • glue

This box is wrapped in old embossed wallpaper. The floral imagery and scale of the design are perfect for the proportions of this box.

The ribbon is made from a photocopy of a handwritten message, "a delicious piece of celebration," which I wrote over and over again to create my own ribbon design. Once photocopied onto a cream paper, I cut it into ½" strips and gave the edge of the paper ribbon a narrow, pale blue watercolor strip.

When your ribbon is dry, cut two lengths long enough to wrap around the box. The bow is a false one you create by cutting two 4" strips and gluing the ends together. Cut a third strip 1" long and shape into an oval. ■

Star Box

Supplies

• cake box • translucent plastic • semi-translucent pale blue Japanese paper • two contrasting ribbons • metal star or other embellishment • glue

The pale blue box is made from a translucent plastic that is lined with pale blue Japanese paper.

Two ¼" contrasting ribbons were wrapped around the box. I used a translucent, mat pale blue and a solid, vintage silver ribbon. This was finished by gluing an old metal star over the ribbons. ■

"Eat me" Box

Supplies

• cake box • patterned pale blue Japanese paper • frosted-glass berries and leaf • pale cream cord • silver thread • aluminum sheet • glue

For this box, I left the bottom uncovered and wrapped the lid with a delicately printed, pale blue Japanese paper.

The frosted-glass berries and leaf are tied together with a pale cream cord, and then tied to the box with four strands of silver thread.

The metal tag, which is cut out from a thin sheet of aluminum, has the words "eat me," stamped into the tag. This was done using old metal printing type. I always stamp the letters first before cutting out the tag. ■

Sparkler Packs

Supplies

• assorted papers • a variety of ribbons and cords • embellishments • silver paint • double-sided tape • glue

These packs are 9" tall x 2¾" wide. The height of your pack will depend on the length of your sparklers.

Create panels of paper 9½" x 6¾" using assorted papers. I chose papers within the color palette of pale blues, creams, buff, and gray, with an accent of silver. I used a mixture of papers–patterned, hand-printed, and hand- and machine-stitched. To save time, make three or four designs and color-copy them.

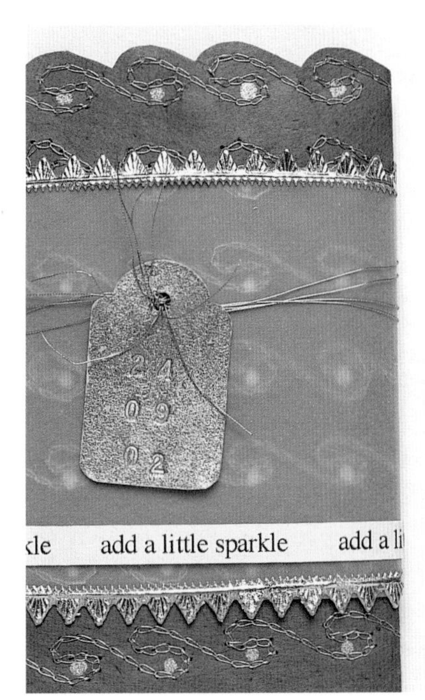

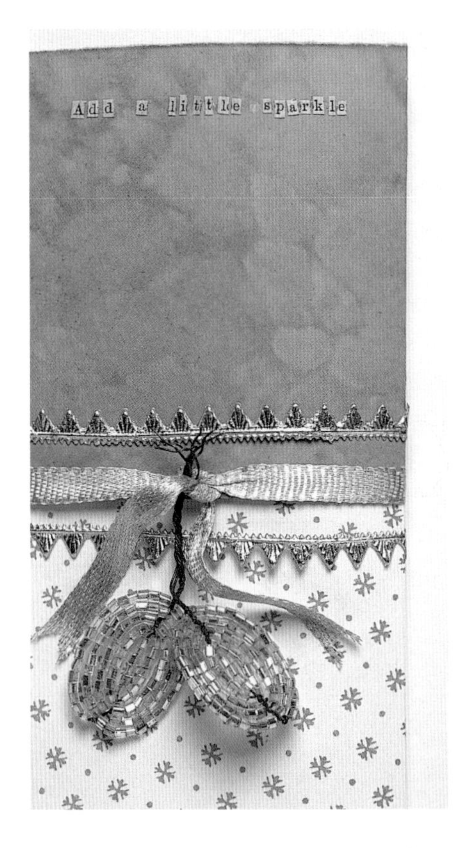

Fold your panel around each sparkler pack, overlapping the back edges and folding the bottom to the back as when wrapping a package. Secure with tape.

Add ribbons, tags, charms, words, beads, metallic threads, and buttons to make each of the packs unique. Highlights of silver paint add a nice sparkling touch. ■

Wreath
page 40

Feather Wreath
Supplies

• wire wreath frame • feather boa • 2 strips of pale blue silk-chiffon ribbon with frayed edges (2¼" x 40") • 2 strips of white silk-chiffon ribbon with frayed edges (3" x 40") • silver paint or metallic silver pen • spray mount

My feather wreath was purchased, but if you can't find the size or color you require, wrap a feather boa around a wire frame.

For the painted silk-chiffon tie, first write out the couple's names or the message that you want to paint onto the fabric. Then, place the strips of pale blue silk chiffon over your message. Due to the translucent nature of the fabric, it should be very easy to trace the letters.

I hand-painted my message with silver paint, but you could also use a metallic pen. Don't use too much paint, as it will run on the fabric.

When the paint is dry, attach the blue chiffon fabric to the strips of white chiffon. Spray mount works well, but you could also use tiny dots of glue or fine running stitches.

Attach your ribbon to the top center of the wreath. ■

Invitations
page 49

When considering the card on which to mount or print your image, take into account the color and the tactile quality of the paper (and do not forget to check the card size against available envelope sizes). For Country Lanes, it had to be quite simple so as not to distract from the daisies. For Color Brights, I used a crisp white, smooth card, which was necessary with all of the color and texture of the image. Antique Whites worked well with a smooth cream background, contrasting with the textured watercolor paper.

Country Lanes Invitation
Supplies

• smooth cardstock (12" x 4") • 2 medium-sized tags (1½" x 2¾") • miniature daisies • tiny price tag (1") • gingham rickrack ribbon • craft glue • pinking shears

I always use luggage labels in my work. For this card, use two medium-sized tags. Glue them so that they overlap with holes aligned. Draw two interlocking circles as a guide for daisy placement. Glue the daisies in place.

Write a message or sentiment on the tiny price tag, and attach it with gingham ribbon threaded through all the holes on the tops of the tags.

Trim your cardstock edges with pinking shears, then fold in half. Glue to the center front of your card. ■

Color Brights Invitation

Supplies

• smooth cardstock (12" x 8½") • old letters and postcards • old stamps • 2 small tags • dried rosebuds • ribbon • silk thread • craft glue • fabric glue

Bundle up your selected old letters and printed ephemera and glue each layer separately to give an informal scattered feel.

Wrap a ribbon around the bundle, choosing a matching or contrasting palette. Stick on old postage stamps to coordinate with the overall effect. Hand-tie a decorative bow and attach two small tags to which you have already applied ornamentation.

For my tags, I hand-embroidered a heart onto one tag, using silk thread.

On the other tag, I glued a rosebud from my special collection.

In order to keep the ribbon in perfect position, I tipped the edges with fabric glue before placing it on the card.

Fold the cardstock in half and glue your bundle to the center front of the card. ■

Antique Whites Invitation

Supplies

• smooth cardstock (11" x 6") • textured watercolor paper • cream metallic paper • small scraps of white and pale blue silk-chiffon fabric • tiny sequins, stars, buttons, or beads • decorative bead or charm • tiny price tag • silver thread • ruler • glue stick

Draw a 3½" square onto a piece of textured watercolor paper to give you guidelines for creating a deckle edge. Lay a ruler up against the inside edge of the pencil line, then tear, pulling the piece of paper you will discard toward you. Repeat along each edge.

Cut out a 3¼" square from white chiffon fabric and fray the edges to make a 3" square. Repeat this with a 2½" square of pale blue chiffon fabric.

With the pale blue fabric on top of the white fabric, attach the fabric squares together with small tacking stitches in the corners.

Next, cut out a heart shape from metallic cream paper that will sit comfortably within the chiffon squares. Gently glue this in place with the glue stick.

Decorate the edge of the heart with tiny sequins, stars, buttons, beads, or anything that fits with your theme.

Fold your cardstock in half and glue your artwork to the front of the card.

For the finishing touch, add a fake closure to the side of the card. I glued a lucky horseshoe bead onto a tiny price tag and tied it onto the card with strands of antique silver thread. ■

Porcelain Pear With a Silver Metal Leaf Place Card

Trace your leaf shape onto a metal sheet, then stamp the name into the metal. I used old metal printer's type to stamp the name, but you can get the same effect by placing a paper over the metal and printing with a ballpoint pen. I used fly-tying scissors to cut out the leaves—these are very small, sharp, and precise. I attached to pear with a twist of silver wire. ■

Seedpod Place Card

The seedpod is from a wisteria plant and has a simple textured white card tag attached with silver wire. Hand-write a guest's name onto the tag. Paint a silver heart on one of the seeds in the pod. ■

Gift Box Place Card

The wrapping paper for the box is a color copy of a blank vintage postcard. I wrote the couples' names, dates, and welcome message onto the paper.

The ribbon also can be made from the photocopy by cutting it into strips that have your own personal message printed on them. The ribbon is edged

with translucent paper cut with vintage pinking shears that I recently acquired while rooting around in a junk shop. ■

Heart Tag Place Card

Draw out your heart shape onto a luggage label and then apply a color wash. When dry, add cut-out letters.

Use a teaspoon to pour melted wax into the heart- area. Add smaller tag with guest's name and a rosebud. ■

Shell Place Card

Paint or write the guest's name onto a strip of white wire-edged ribbon that you knot in the middle and glue in place at the top of the shell. Sprinkle silver dragées onto the shell for your guests' delight! ■

Country Lanes
Place Name Settings

Supplies

• terra-cotta pots (2" diameter) • small wire basket pots • small-leafed plants, such as moss or thyme • twigs • wire-edged ribbon • vintage plant labels • copper sheeting or copper paper • sage-green paint • metallic paint or pen • double-sided tape

The terra-cotta pots have a very pale sage green color wash to fit in with the color palette of this story. I lined the wire basket pots with moss to stop the soil from falling out. I would recommend planting up these pots at least a couple of weeks before the

wedding to let the plants settle in—just remember to water them!

In this case, I have used "mind your own business," as I felt the pale green worked well with this story and the size of the leaves was in perfect scale with the twig flagpoles. You could use a variety of other fillings—moss, thyme, any of the small-leafed sedums—or small flowering plants such as violas, tiny alpine strawberries, and Bellis (daisies).

For the name flags, I painted the names onto the wire-edged ribbon using metallic paint. If you like, you could use a metallic pen or brush pen. I then attached them to the twigs with a small strip of double-sided tape to secure them. Other name tags shown here are vintage plant labels, which came from one of my favorite stores in New York, The French General.

The copper metal tags which record the date are stamped using old metal printing type. If you do not have anything with which to imprint the dates, use copper paper and print the information onto the tag. ■

Thank-you Cards

page 54

Country Lanes
Thank-you Card

Supplies

• cardstock • paper strips (2" x 1/5") • metallic rings threaded onto wire • glass heart • pressed daisy • pale green watercolor paint • melted wax • instant-bond glue

Another discovery from one of my favorite New York stores, The French General, was metallic rings threaded onto wire, which I then bent into a heart shape. You could do something similar by stringing beads onto wire.

I made a card from the cardstock, and I attached the heart shape to the front with five tiny tacking stitches.

For the green band below the heart, I wrote, "with . . . and thanks," onto a strip of paper, leaving a space for a tiny heart shape painted onto a small piece of sea-washed glass.

I then gave the strip of paper a color wash of pale green watercolor paint. When this was dry, I dipped it in melted wax to form a thin coating.

The glass heart was glued onto the gap left in the message. The finishing touch is the pressed daisy (or a flower from your wedding) glued onto the card at the end of the wax panel. ■

Color Brights Thank-you Card

Supplies

• white cardstock (14" x 9") • thick pale cream paper (4" x 7") • scraps of silk-chiffon fabric (4" x 4") • brightly colored frayed silks and ribbons • silk thread • scraps of patterned paper • printed matter (to cut out words) • copper metal sheet • pressed anemone flower • metallic silver paint • double-sided tape • fabric glue • spray mount • very fine scissors or craft knife

For the central panel of artwork, take a piece of thick pale cream paper and lightly sketch out your design. On the bottom third of the panel, glue a 1" square of patterned paper above the area where you are going to stitch the heart square. Stitch the heart with silk threads.

Next, attach the panels of brightly colored frayed silks and ribbons with a running stitch in a silk thread. Glue three tiny squares of patterned paper on your design with fabric glue.

To add a little contrast and sparkle, I cut up strips of thin copper metal about 1⁄16" wide. Before cutting up the metal sheet, attach a strip of double-sided tape to the back of it. Stick the copper strips onto your design.

The top half of the card is made up of silk-chiffon fabric. A pressed anemone flower was centrally glued on using spray mount. The fabric was then attached to the panel at the top with a running stitch. The ribbons were glued on at the top and bottom of the chiffon using a fabric glue or dry glue, as you don't want this to stain the ribbon.

With very fine scissors or craft knife, cut out letters to spell "Thank You" from an old book or other printed matter. Stick the letters on with fabric glue. The finishing touch is just a tad of metallic paint dusted on the stamens of the pressed flower and on the paper of the stitched heart.

Fold the cardstock in half to make a card 7" x 9". Glue your artwork on the front center of card. ■

Antique Whites Thank-you Card

Supplies

• watercolor paper (8" x 5") • tracing paper (¾" x 4") • Chinese funeral paper (1½" square) • lace strip (4" x ¾") • vintage stitched star • spray mount • fabric glue • pencil • ruler

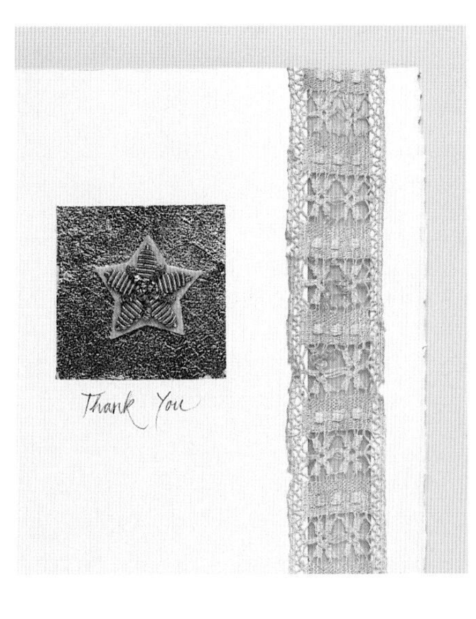

Create a deckle edge on both 4" sides of the watercolor paper by placing a ruler along the edge and slowly pulling the strip of paper to be discarded toward you.

In order to create the translucent band that the strip of lace sits on, cut out a ¾" wide strip about ½" in from the right-hand side of the card. Next, glue a strip of tracing paper to the back of the two pieces of the card. Gently spray-mount the back of your lace strip and position on the front of your card over the strip of tracing paper.

For the star square, I cut out a 1½" square of Chinese funeral paper, and attached this on with spray mount. I attached the vintage stitched star with fabric glue. "Thank You" is written in pencil to be in keeping with the overall soft tones of the card. Fold your paper in half to make your card. ■

Bouquet
page 64

White Rose Bouquet
Supplies
• bouquet of roses • 2 pieces of heavy cardstock (12" x 12") • silk thread • old mother-of-pearl buttons • silk-organza ribbon with frayed edges • double-sided tape • glue gun and glue sticks

A tight bouquet of English garden roses is framed by a ring of wrapped silk and buttons.

To make the collar, cut out two rings from cardstock, one 10½" in diameter and the other 9½". I have added interest to the shape of this ring by curving the edges. This undulation gives more beauty and movement to the silk thread border.

Take the smaller of the card rings and cover the back with a strip of double-sided tape. Then, start to wrap the silk thread around the card. To help the flow of the wrapping, draw directional lines around the ring. Do this very lightly with a pencil, as you do not want the marks to show through. This will enable you to lay the thread down and cover the backing card as neatly as possible.

When you have finished wrapping, glue the silk-wrapped card onto the larger ring, leaving a ¼" edge around the ring for borders of buttons.

Use a glue gun to attach the mother-of-pearl buttons around the ring.

The finishing touch is the frayed edging of silk organza, which is ruched around the edge of the outer ring. Attach this using double-sided tape. ■

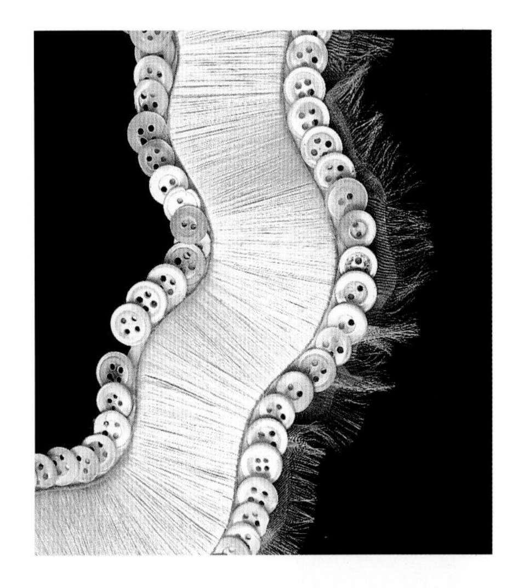

Celebration Paper Wreath
Supplies
• heavy cardstock • cream paper • hand-dyed silk ribbon • glue

Cut template from cardstock to the size you would like your wreath to be, in this case 14" diameter.

For the leaves, type in the bridal couple's names on your computer, using a pale moss-green type. Repeat the names over and over, leaving enough space between each line to draw a leaf shape around the names. Print out onto cream paper.

Trace a leaf outline around each set of names. I drew a line down the middle of the traced overlay leaf in order to make certain that the names were straight and ran down the center of the leaf. Cut out leaves and glue to cardstock wreath. I reduced the last three leaves at the top of the wreath on each side gradually to get a tapering effect.

Tie a bow from silk ribbon and place on bottom center of wreath. ■

Ribbon Wreath

Supplies

• 8" strips of frayed ribbon • 10" wire wreath • vintage paper daisies • wild grass • decorative ribbon • glue

Tie strips of frayed ribbon to your wire wreath frame.

For the posy at the top of the wreath, I glued on vintage paper daisies with a bow glued to the top. The finishing touch was the wild grass, which I just tucked in with the daisies. ■

Welcome Moss Door Wreath

Supplies

• 16" oasis ring • moss • white chrysanthemum daisies • wire (¼" x 3') • floral wire • wide decorative ribbon • wire cutters

Soak oasis ring in water and cover with moss. Attach the moss with 2" pieces of wire bent into 'U' shapes.

Decorate with white chrysanthemum daisies. Wrap the 2" stems with floral wire so that they don't snap when being pushed into the oasis.

Make a bow around top of wreath with wide decorative ribbon. ■

Staircase Garland

Supplies

• hydrangeas • enough white and ice blue silk-chiffon fabric to drape along staircase • blue-and-white silk-chiffon ribbon • cardstock • melted wax • water vials • silver paint or silver metallic pen • double-sided tape

This beautiful staircase was very simply decorated with white and ice blue silk-chiffon swags.

Make paper cones by rolling card-stock into cone shapes, and securing at the back with double-sided tape.

Melt wax and let cool. Cut out small strips of wax and press them in a random pattern over cones for a translucent effect.

Attach the paper cones at regular intervals along the railing.

Place hydrangea blooms into small water vials, which are available from your local florist. Carefully place the hydrangeas into the cones.

Write the bridal couple's names, wedding date, or other romantic message in silver on the blue-and-white chiffon ribbon. Attach this ribbon to the cone at the bottom of the staircase. ■

Confetti Cones

page 69

Country Lanes Cone

Supplies

• heavy patterned paper • narrow gingham checked ribbon • tiny leaves and daisies • paper butterfly • double-sided tape • craft glue

Make three cones from your heavy paper by cutting out a large circle from the paper and then dividing it into thirds (like you would cut a pie). Roll each piece into a cone and secure at the back with double-sided tape.

Glue the gingham ribbon around the top of the cone and embellish it with the daisies and leaves. For the finishing touch, add a paper butterfly. ■

Color Brights Cone

Supplies

• photocopy of handwritten lettering • copper metal sheet • ribbon scraps • pressed flower • crepe paper • double-sided tape • spray mount • craft glue • pinking shears

Make a cone from the handwriting photocopy.

Cut a 1"-wide strip of crepe paper that will fit around the top edge of the cone.

Glue it to the inside edge, leaving about ¾" showing above the cone. Make narrow cuts almost down to the cone, creating a fringed look. Cut a ½"-wide strip from your copper metal sheet, pink the top edge, and glue around the top of the cone.

Spray-mount the flower in place and finish with two scraps of ribbon. ■

Antique Whites Cone

Supplies

• handmade gray paper with silver machine-stitched design • white sheer ribbon (2" wide) • vintage silver metal trim • silver star or snowflake • vintage star button • double-sided tape • fabric glue • snowflake paper punch

Make a paper cone from the gray handmade paper.

Cut a piece of the sheer ribbon to fit around the top edge of the cone and secure in place. Glue the silver trim to the top and bottom of the ribbon and then add the silver star and button.

Fill with desired confetti, in this case, a mixture of rice, pale blue paper snowflakes, and translucent iridescent hearts. Note: the paper snowflakes were made using a snowflake paper punch. ■

Candles & Lanterns

page 72-74

Spring Country Lantern

Fill base of hurricane vase with moss and add a candle. Arrange more moss around candle and add daisies.

For the butterflies, I photocopied vintage etched images and then gave them a light color wash. Glue paper butterflies to outside of lantern. ■

Seascape Lantern

Fill base of hurricane vase with very fine pale sand. Add a candle and a bit more sand. Scatter painted sea-

washed chalk and pale blue pebbles around the sand. For the finishing touch, add some silver dragées. ■

Summer Bright Lantern

Fill an old canning jar about 2" deep with sand laced with pink glitter. Prop colorful candles up in the sand. ■

Daisy Votive

These pressed daisies are simply glued onto the outside of the glass votive holder, using spray mount. ■

Beaded Votive

Glass beads are threaded onto a cord, which is then glued to the glass votive holder. Knot the cord randomly between the beads and the cord becomes an interesting decorative element as well. ■

Fringed Votive

Make a fringed crepe-paper band to fit around a glass votive holder. Enhance the band with a pinked strip of copper metal sheeting. ■

Terra-cotta Pots

These were on our wedding tables, four of each. These old pots have a color wash of pale green paint to knock back the terra-cotta.

The bottoms of the pots are sealed with masking tape and then filled with moist sand. Fill up to about 2" from the top, allowing for the moss topping.

Position the candles, and allow sand to dry. This will set, holding the candles tightly in position.

The day before you want to use the candles, top off with damp moss. ■

Frosted-heart Votive

The glass was frosted using etched-glass spray. Simply mask off the area you want to leave unfrosted. I attached a paper heart shape with low-tack tape. I also masked off the lip of the votive. Then I gently sprayed with three coats of etched-glass spray.

When dry, remove masking. ■

Bark Candle

This candle was wrapped with silver-birch bark. Glue the two ends together with instant-bond glue, and then tie with silver thread. For a little sparkle, a snowberry and glass leaf adornment were added. ■

Country Lanterns

Supplies

• small glass jars • wire • wire cutters • needle-nosed pliers

Apart from the candles on the tables, we also had little lanterns hanging in the trees. These were made from glass French yogurt pots. (Yes we ate an awful lot of yogurt before the wedding, luckily it's good for you!) Baby food jars would also work.

In order to hang them from the trees, wire was wrapped around the lip of the jar and 12" wire handles were attached with delicate little twists and twirls at the end. Use pliers to bend and twist the wire.

Note: Make the handles longer than you think in case you need to twist the wire around a twig rather than just hanging it. ■

Seed Packet

Supplies

• unbleached greaseproof (glassine) paper • pale green cord • tan hole reinforcements • desired fillings • double-sided tape • hole punch

For each packet, cut a piece of the unbleached greaseproof (glassine) paper 10" x 5".

Fold the short ends to the back and overlap ½". Crease edges and then secure them back with double-sided tape.

Next, fold up the bottom toward the back ½" and secure as above.

Fill your packet with lime-green dragées, Jordan almonds, chocolate-coated coffee beans, or anything else you might desire.

Fold the top edge over to the back about ½" and crease well. Punch a hole through the top of the bag and add a tan reinforcement over the hole.

Cut a 10" piece from cord. Loop the cord through the hole and secure with a slipknot. ■

Daisy Print Tag

Supplies

• medium tag • 6 tiny daisy buttons • green watercolor paint • copper metallic paint • printed material • wording from a seed packet • thin wire or thread for attaching tag • spray mount • glue • hole punch

Using your tag as a pattern, trace and cut a piece of printed material to cover the tag. Remove the reinforcement from the tag and glue the printed piece to the tag with spray mount.

Punch a hole at the original hole site and reattach the reinforcement. Cut a small strip of wording from the seed packet, and glue to the bottom of the tag that will embellish the favor.

Give your tag a light wash of green watercolor. When dry, glue on the daisy buttons and highlight their centers with metallic copper paint. ■

Postcard Tag

Supplies

• old postcard with stamp • 2 copper daisies • bridal couple's names and wedding date cut from printed type • tan hole reinforcement • thin wire or thread for attaching tag • glue • hole punch

Cut a tag from an old postcard, making certain to include the stamp on the tag.

Punch a hole in the top and cover with a tan reinforcement.

Glue on the couple's names and wedding date, and then attach the copper daisies. ■

Seed Tag

Supplies

• photocopy of seed packet • flat seed • small pressed leaf • tan hole reinforcement • thin wire or thread for attaching tag • glue • hole punch

Cut a tag shape from your seed packet photocopy. Note: If you photocopy onto cream paper rather than white, it gives a more antique appearance.

Punch a hole in the top and cover with a tan reinforcement. Glue on your seed and leaf. ■

Colorful Bags

Supplies

• wool felt squares • ribbons, cords, or decorative wire for handles • embellishments for front of bags (ribbons, buttons, beads, fabric flowers) • tissue paper • matching threads • fabric glue • pinking shears

Cut two 3" squares of felt and place one on top of the other. Sew a seam along three sides. If you want, you can trim the edges with pinking shears.

Stitch your desired handle to the top of the bag. Attach whatever embellishments you choose with either fabric glue or tiny stitches.

This little butterfly was made using wire-edged ribbon. Cut a 3" piece and roll up to form the body. Attach to bag.

Then, cut four 1" pieces of ribbon. Fold over the corners on one end on each piece to form a point, and attach wings to body. The antennae were pieces of pale green cord that were positioned on the bag with glue.

Fill your bags with colorful tissue paper and whatever "surprise" you would like to include. ■

Accessories

page 88-93

Flower Girls' Shoes

Supplies

• shoes • fabric that matches dress or other coordinating fabric • tracing paper • buckles and trims • glue • pinking shears

For the lining, take a piece of tracing paper small enough to squeeze into the shoe but big enough to allow you to trace the shape of the inner sole. If you are really lucky, your shoe's inner sole may be removable and you can cover it. If not, make a template from your tracing and cut out from your chosen fabric with pinking shears. Lightly glue this to the inner sole. The buckle and trim are simply glued to the shoes. ■

Millie's Ribbon Wreath

Supplies

• Plastic embroidery hoop (6") • various ribbons (½" wide and 2" wide) • glue gun and glue sticks

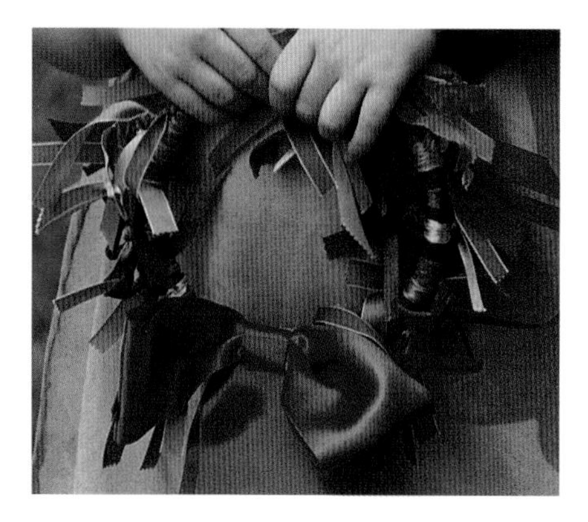

Cut many 6" lengths of ribbon. Tie ribbons to hoop by folding in half and threading ends through the loop of the ribbon. As you tie the ribbons on, bunch them up together in order to get as dense a concentration of ribbons as possible. You could vary the pattern of the ribbon collar by just using two colors and tying them in 1" bands to create a stripe. Also, a looser feel could be achieved by varying the lengths of ribbon.

Cut a 36" length from the 2" ribbon. Make a bow and glue to the wreath. ■

Ring Box

Supplies

• ring box (2½" x 2" x 1½") • pale cream, slightly textured paper • blue silk ribbon • vintage silver paper trim • pressed forget-me-nots • lavender flowers • sesame seeds • printed matter • silver paint • spray mount • craft glue • pvc glue

For the ring box, I covered an existing box with pale cream paper.

For the edging, first attach the blue ribbon. Note: If you are using a thin or silk ribbon, just glue at either end as you do not want the glue to stain the ribbon and leave a watermark. Next, the silver paper trim was glued onto the ribbon. Again, use the glue sparingly.

For the lid, position and attach pressed forget-me-not flowers with spray mount. Paint on silver stems.

Glue on the lavender flowers, sesame seeds, and cut-out type. ■

Tied the Knot Pillow

Supplies

• cream felt (two 5" squares) • ruffled edging (20") • silver or cream cord (8") • glue

The pleasure of this pillow is the mixture of rich materials with the contrasting simple type.

You can either hand-print your message or iron on the type, it is up to you. Print your message on one of the felt squares.

Make the pillow by using two 5" squares of fabric. Pin a ruffled edging to the top fabric (the one you have printed on), with raw edge of ruffle matching raw edge of fabric. Baste.

Place the two squares with right sides together and sew around the edges, leaving an opening for turning.

Turn and stuff the pillow, then sew the opening closed.

Stitch an 8" cream or silver cord to the center of the pillow to use for tying on the rings. ■

Moss Ring Pillow

Supplies

• oasis • moss • floral wire • daisies • floral wire • ribbon • wire cutters

Cut soaked oasis to the required shape, minus an inch all the way around to allow for the moss.

Pin the moss to the oasis, using floral wires bent into 'U's. Position the daisies and attach stems to the pillow in the same manner.

Using floral pins, pin where the flower head meets the stem and where the two stems cross. ■

Pot with Silver Birds

Supplies

• metal sheet • tracing paper • gilded paper • metallic paint • ballpoint pen • tin snips • craft glue

For the "messengers," the silver birds, first sketch out your design onto tracing paper. Place over the metal sheet and trace through with a ballpoint pen. Cut out your bird images with tin snips.

For the feathers, I used gilded paper and metallic paint. You can also create another finish to the metal by simply scratching at the surface with a sharp craft knife.

Attach the paper feathers and gifts in their beaks with glue. ■

Silver Fruit Boxes

Supplies

• tissue paper • computer-printed saying • clear removable tape • pinking shears

Cut squares of tissue paper big enough to wrap around your gift, allowing extra for tying. You can only work this out by playing around with different sizes of paper. In this case, I cut out 7" squares of tissue.

For the next step, I made a great discovery while experimenting with my computer and ink-jet printer. I printed out rows of type listing the names of the happy couple. Once these were printed, I took pieces of clear tape and gently laid them over the lines of type. When I lifted the tape off of the paper, the type transfers onto the tape and can be easily placed on the edge of the tissue.

Note: Experiment with your printer to make certain this works. The type might not lift off as well if you have a laser printer.

For the finishing touch, pink the edges of the tissue paper.

There are two things that are so nice about this little trick. First, you cannot see the tape on the tissue, just the type. Second, you'll notice that as you wrap the tissue around your gift, the edges will have a slight stiffness to them, yet will stay smooth in contrast to the crumpled tissue. ■

Cufflink Box

Supplies

• ring box • textured paper • green hearts on stems • ribbon • dark green moss • double-sided tape

I covered an existing ring box with textured paper. The edging was achieved by placing a fine strip of double-sided tape around the top edge and bottom of the box. I then placed the seed heads (green hearts on stems) onto the tape, and wrapped a length of ribbon around the stems to finish off the look.

An additional strip of ribbon around the top balances it out.

Apart from the delicious gift inside, the other surprise within is the lining—dark green moss, which I love to work with. ■

Photo Albums

page 104–105

Country Lanes Photo Album Cover

Supplies

• plain photo album • stretched paper • watercolor paint • cream ribbon (1"-wide) • pale green ribbon (¼"-wide) • assorted decorations from wedding theme • vintage fabric daisy • double-sided tape • glue • pinking shears

For the album shown here, I first painted the watercolor strips onto stretched paper. Once dry, I then covered a plain album cover, using double-sided tape to secure.

The decorations consist of elements from the Country Lanes Wedding. You want this to be a reminder of your beautiful day, so pull out the elements of the decorations that are most pertinent to you.

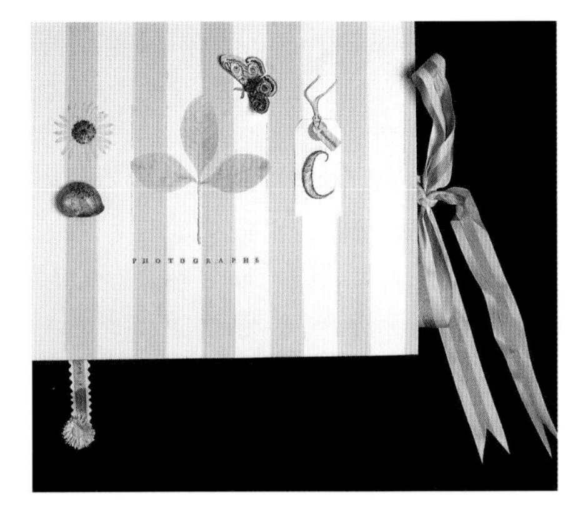

Experiment with the arrangements of your decorations, and then secure to album cover with spray mount.

I wanted the ribbon to echo the stripes of the cover, so I glued two different ribbons together, cream and pale green.

For the page marker, the ribbon has a paper edging to it. This not only gives it an interesting twist, but also gives it more substance.

Mount your pale green ribbon onto a strip of paper that is a little wider than the ribbon. Pink the edges of the paper. The ribbon is decorated with the names of the bride and groom and finished off with a vintage fabric daisy. ■

Photo Album Page

Supplies

• pale green, transparent handmade paper • pressed fern leaf • pressed daisies • printed matter • metallic lettering spelling the bridal couple's names • spray mount • glue

Attach the pressed fern leaf to the actual scrapbook page with the spray mount.

Cut a piece of handmade paper the same size as the scrapbook page. Use spray mount to attach to page over the top of the leaf. You should be able to see the leaf through the paper.

From printed matter, cut out the words "marriage of" and glue to the top center of the album page.

Glue the metallic letters spelling out the bridal couple's names onto the page. Using silver, copper, and gold lettering adds a nice touch.

I attached the daisies randomly over the page, using spray mount. ■

Copper Album Tag

Supplies

• copper metal sheet • pressed daisy • copper metal daisy • two tiny price tags • one small tag • tan hole reinforcement • metallic copper paint • thin copper wire • old metal printer's type • spray mount • glue • tin snips

This is the tag I used for my wedding album. I cut a 5" x 2" tag from a copper metal sheet.

I punched a hole in the top of the tag and covered it with a tan hole reinforcement. I then threaded a thin copper wire through the hole to use for attaching my tag to the photo album.

Then, I spray-mounted a pressed daisy to the center of my copper tag and highlighted the center with copper paint.

Our names were stamped into the tag, using old metal printer's type. Placing a piece of paper on the metal and printing with ballpoint pen also works well.

I cut out words from small printed type, spelling "Wedding" and "Album," and glued the words onto the tiny price tags.

On a small tag, I glued a metal daisy, then attached all three tags to the copper wire. ■

Picture Frames

page 107 & 109

Color Brights Picture Frame

Supplies

• heavy art paper (6½" square) • foam-core board (6½" square) • metallic oil pastels • a variety of silk thread • photocopies of vintage postcards • scraps of silk chiffon • assorted beads, sequins, ribbons, papers, and copper strips • dried rosebud • fabric flower • metallic bronzing powder • glue • pinking shears • craft knife

First, sketch out your design before committing to the art paper. I used a fairly heavy paper. You need something thick enough to withstand handling, but not so thick that you can't stitch through the paper.

The outside measurements of this frame are 6½" square with a 2½" opening in the center. Once you have cut out your frame, draw on your design.

For this frame, I first applied the areas of flat color using metallic oil pastels. I drew a heart onto the bottom left-hand square (which was painted) and then stitched around it, making stripes with various colors of silk thread and letting the paint show through the heart relief.

I glued a photocopy of a vintage postcard to the top-center, top-right, and bottom-right squares of the frame. I then hand-stitched a heart on the top-center square.

The top square of silk fabric is decorated with sequins studded with bronze glass beads.

For the top-left and bottom-right squares, I attached a frayed-edged square of silk chiffon by lightly tacking down in each corner.

The other squares were embellished with ribbons, pinked paper and copper metal sheets, beads, a rose-bud, and a fabric flower. Attach using a small amount of glue for positioning, then secure ribbons and papers tightly around the back of the frame.

The final touch is a bit of gilding, using the metallic bronzing powders.

When your artwork is finished, mount onto foam-core board, which is 6½" square with a 3" square opening.

Tidy up the edge of the frame with either a wash of harmonizing paint, or glue a ribbon around the edge just to give it a finished appearance.

Attach a 4" card backing over the opening. Glue on three sides at the very edge, thus allowing you to slip your photograph in and out. ■

Button Heart Frame

Supplies

• heavy cardstock • foam-core board • old mother-of-pearl buttons • craft knife • glue gun and glue sticks.

First, work out the size of the opening you require for your chosen image. This will dictate the size of your heart.

I used a fairly thick cardstock for the backing board, as the buttons will be quite heavy by the time you have finished layering them. Cut out your heart shape and opening from the cardstock with a craft knife.

In order to give the heart the appearance of floating in the frame, you will need to cut out a heart from foam-core board, which is ½" smaller all the way around and ½" larger than your opening.

Glue the foam-core board heart onto the back of your cardstock heart.

Before you glue the buttons down, play around with the positioning, as you may change your mind over the composition. A glue gun works great for attaching the buttons.

Note: If your old mother-of-pearl buttons are looking a little dull, soak them in milk for one hour, rinse with warm soapy water, and gently buff them dry. This will bring back their original luster. ■

Keepsake Box

page 110–111

Keepsake Box

Supplies

• balsa-wood box • liming wax • pearl buttons • vintage silver metal ribbon • vintage silver hands • thick watercolor paper • instant-bond glue

This old balsa-wood box has just been waiting for the right project! To soften the look of the wood, I limed it. This gives it a slightly cooler hue, which works well with the pearly buttons and vintage silver.

For the button heart, cut out the required shape from thick watercolor paper. This slightly textured paper is a nice contrast to the smooth wooden box.

The edging of vintage buttons is attached, using instant-bond glue.

The vintage metal hands are a lucky junk shop find and are the perfect heart holder.

The ribbon, which is vintage silver metal, is glued on to the box, as are all the elements. ■

Sarah Lugg

ABOUT THE AUTHOR

Combining a lifelong passion for collecting, meticulous attention to detail, and an exquisite artistic sensibility, British artist Sarah Lugg creates intimate works of art that have won her an international following. Her distinctive artwork incorporates natural treasures and found objects that most of us rarely notice. Tiny leaves, delicate shells, miniature flower buds, a snippet of antique fabric . . . all come together in perfect harmony under her practiced hand and artistic eye.

Sarah's mixed-media collages convey a spiritual message that transcends their common origins or diminutive scale. Within the context of her work, the tiniest fragment of nature is endowed with content, symbolism, and spirituality. Her creations present the common from an uncommon perspective and offer a glimpse of a world with which she believes we are fast losing touch.

ACKNOWLEDGMENTS

THANKS TO THE FOLLOWING PEOPLE FOR THEIR HELP WITH THIS BOOK:

Bo Hotston for her incredible creative spirit and dedication to this project, outstanding ability to work all hours, love, and for being bossy!

Patrick Regan for his way with words

Caroline Arber and Mo for capturing the moments on film so beautifully

Jo Packham for saying yes

Carmen Tarnowski for arranging the location, coping with all the mess, and appearing at one of our lowest points with a huge tray of bacon sandwiches!

Helen Powell for letting me raid her home for fabulous props

Simon Richards for his floral vision

Anne Wilson for bunting, stitching, and moral support

Lisa Ashcraft for holding the fort while I was so preoccupied with the book

Robert Muller for wheeling and dealing

A big thank-you to Eva and Richard Little who so graciously loaned their home

Denise Fiedler of Bravura for the following designs:
Beaded S and R, p.85; Brag books, p.106; Felt bags, p.81; Flower girls' shoes, p.88–89; Ribbon wreath, p.68; Ribbon wreath, p.90; Ring pillows, p.92; Shawls, p.87; Wooden boxes, p.78

Kaari Meng of The French General for the following designs:
Bead strung threads, p.72; Message in a bottle, p.86

PROJECT/PHOTO REFERENCE

PROJECTS	PHOTOS	MAKES
Amaretto Biscuits	30	116–117
Antique Whites Cone	69	128
Antique Whites Invitation	49	121
Antique Whites Thank-you Card	54	124–125
Bark Candle	73	129
Beaded Votive	73	129
Button Daisy	19	113
Button Heart Frame	109	137
Card Ring	19	113–114
Celebration Paper Wreath	68	125–126
Collage Napkin Ring	31	118
Color Brights Cone	69	127
Color Brights Invitation	49	121
Color Brights Picture Frame	107	136
Color Brights Thank-you Card	54	124
Colorful Bags	81	131–132
Copper Album Tag	105	135–136
Copper Heart Napkin Ring	31	117
Country Lanes Cone	69	127
Country Lanes Invitation	49	120
Country Lanes Lanterns	74	130
Country Lanes Photo Album Cover	104–105	134–135
Country Lanes Place Name Settings	52–53	123
Country Lanes Thank-you Card	54	123–124
Cufflink Box	100	134
Daisy Print Tag	78	130–131
Daisy Tag Sapling	20	115
Daisy Votive	72	129
"Eat me" Box	38	119
Embossed Box	38	118
Feather Wreath	40	120
Fern Tag Sapling	20	114–115
Flower Girls' Shoes	88–89	132
Fringed Napkin Ring	31	117–118

PROJECTS	PHOTOS	MAKES
Fringed Votive	72	129
Frosted-heart Votive	72	129
Gift Box Place Card	51	122
Heart Tag Place Card	51	122
Keepsake Box	110–111	137
Map Tag Sapling	20	114
Metal Ring	19	113
Millie's Ribbon Wreath	90	132
Moss Ring Pillow	93	133
Photo Album Page	105	135
Porcelain Pear With a Silver Metal Leaf Place Card	51	122
Postcard Tag	78	131
Pot with Silver Birds	96	133
Ribbon Knot	19	113
Ribbon Wreath	68	126
Ring Box	92	132
Seascape Lantern	73	128
Seed Packet	21, 78	130
Seed Tag	21, 78	131
Seedpod Place Card	51	122
Shell Place Card	51	122
Silver Fruit Boxes	99	134
Sparkler Packs	39	119
Spring Country Lantern	72	128
Staircase Garland	69	126–127
Star Box	38	118–119
Stitched-leaf Tag Sapling	20	115
Summer Bright Lantern	72	128
Table Numbers	26–27, 29	116
Terra-cotta Pots	73	129
Tied the Knot Pillow	92	133
Welcome Moss Door Wreath	68	126
White Rose Bouquet	64	125
Window Dressing	26–28	116

Metric Equivalency Charts

mm-millimetres cm-centimetres
inches to millimetres and centimetres

inches	mm	cm	inches	cm	inches	cm
⅛	3	0.3	9	22.9	30	76.2
¼	6	0.6	10	25.4	31	78.7
⅜	10	1.0	11	27.9	32	81.3
½	13	1.3	12	30.5	33	83.8
⅝	16	1.6	13	33.0	34	86.4
¾	19	1.9	14	35.6	35	88.9
⅞	22	2.2	15	38.1	36	91.4
1	25	2.5	16	40.6	37	94.0
1¼	32	3.2	17	43.2	38	96.5
1½	38	3.8	18	45.7	39	99.1
1¾	44	4.4	19	48.3	40	101.6
2	51	5.1	20	50.8	41	104.1
2½	64	6.4	21	53.3	42	106.7
3	76	7.6	22	55.9	43	109.2
3½	89	8.9	23	58.4	44	111.8
4	102	10.2	24	61.0	45	114.3
4½	114	11.4	25	63.5	46	116.8
5	127	12.7	26	66.0	47	119.4
6	152	15.2	27	68.6	48	121.9
7	178	17.8	28	71.1	49	124.5
8	203	20.3	29	73.7	50	127.0

yards to metres

yards	metres	yards	metres	yards	metres	yards	metres	yards	metres
⅛	0.11	2⅛	1.94	4⅛	3.77	6⅛	5.60	8⅛	7.43
¼	0.23	2¼	2.06	4¼	3.89	6¼	5.72	8¼	7.54
⅜	0.34	2⅜	2.17	4⅜	4.00	6⅜	5.83	8⅜	7.66
½	0.46	2½	2.29	4½	4.11	6½	5.94	8½	7.77
⅝	0.57	2⅝	2.40	4⅝	4.23	6⅝	6.06	8⅝	7.89
¾	0.69	2¾	2.51	4¾	4.34	6¾	6.17	8¾	8.00
⅞	0.80	2⅞	2.63	4⅞	4.46	6⅞	6.29	8⅞	8.12
1	0.91	3	2.74	5	4.57	7	6.40	9	8.23
1⅛	1.03	3⅛	2.86	5⅛	4.69	7⅛	6.52	9⅛	8.34
1¼	1.14	3¼	2.97	5¼	4.80	7¼	6.63	9¼	8.46
1⅜	1.26	3⅜	3.09	5⅜	4.91	7⅜	6.74	9⅜	8.57
1½	1.37	3½	3.20	5½	5.03	7½	6.86	9½	8.69
1⅝	1.49	3⅝	3.31	5⅝	5.14	7⅝	6.97	9⅝	8.80
1¾	1.60	3¾	3.43	5¾	5.26	7¾	7.09	9¾	8.92
1⅞	1.71	3⅞	3.54	5⅞	5.37	7⅞	7.20	9⅞	9.03
2	1.83	4	3.66	6	5.49	8	7.32	10	9.14

INDEX